THE JUDICIAL VETO

THE JUDICIAL VETO

BY

HORACE A. DAVIS

BOSTON AND NEW YORK
HOUGHTON MIFFLIN COMPANY
The Riverside Press Cambridge
1914

112436

PREFACE

THE three essays on judicial review which make up this book contribute each its share to the conclusion that deciding the constitutionality of statutes is a political and not a legal function. The tendency of courts as well as laymen to disregard this fundamental principle and to view the whole subject as a branch of jurisprudence has led to an intolerable political situation. That some change will be made becomes increasingly evident.

The conviction that the subject, technical though it may be, is of vital and immediate importance to the body politic is my reason for publishing these essays. The first chapter attempts to sketch in untechnical language the present situation and the present tendency; the second proposes a common-sense remedy; the third is an historical study of the origin of judicial review in the federal Supreme Court. Under a strictly logical arrangement, the historical essay should come first; but its value is almost wholly academic, and it seemed better to give the more practical essays precedence.

"Annulment of Legislation by the Supreme Court" (chapter III) was published in *The American Political Science Review* and is republished with slight revision through the courtesy of its editor. The other two essays are new.

HORACE A. DAVIS.

BROOKLINE, 1914.

CONTENTS

THE JUDICIAL VETO

CHAPTER I

EXTRA-CONSTITUTIONAL LAW

CITIZENS and legislatures alike have been besieged in recent years by proposals for constitutional amendment; yet in all the discussion aroused by income tax, workingmen's compensation, and countless other reforms, the fact has virtually escaped notice that our constitutions are actually being amended almost from week to week — often most emphatically against our will. The agency through which such amendment is taking place is judicial decision.

From colonial days the courts have claimed the power to interpret all written constitutions, and such power has, though not without some early misgivings, been liberally conceded to them. Now the power to interpret practically includes the power to amend; for every *erroneous* decision gives a new twist to the constitution, imposes some limitation on it, and, for better or for worse, changes its meaning for the purpose at least of the case decided. We all know that practically courts do decide Dartmouth College [1] and Ives [2] cases and render Dred Scott opinions, and that it takes a formal constitutional amendment, or a war, to undo the mischief.

It is only recently that this situation has attracted popular attention and become the subject of political criticism. I shall consider in another chapter the possibility of devising better means of deciding constitutional questions; the purpose of this chapter is simply to point out that the principal effect of such a scheme, whatever form it may take, would be, not to review judicial action or to amend the constitution, but *to prevent the courts from amending it.*

The origin of the judicial power of constitutional review has recently been the subject of considerable discussion. [3] How did the courts get the right to declare a law unconstitutional and void? No such power is in terms granted by the federal Constitution itself, or by the state constitutions; nor is there any logical necessity why the opinion of the judiciary, one of the three branches of the government, should override the action of another, the legis-

3 cong.

ending in er. = donner.
        ir   partir
        oir   avoir
        re = être
              dire
              faire

Il a parlé
j'ai aimé   I lovely

donne-je   ↗ 8 8

Boutin
j'ai vendu mes livres
aux professeurs dé la université

déjà = already
bien - well.

26�?6 - 3?6

pouvons-nous manger maintenant

Est-ce que vous parlez le
français bien?

Oui je parle la langue française
très bien.

J'ai parlé le français pour
beaucoup des ans.

de le = du
de les = des.

— — — — — — —

Le monsieur est à la maison!

Les hommes donnent
leurs bêtes au professeur.
Les femmes sont ici dans
la salle à manger.
Les garçons ont parti pour
l'école.
Est-ce que j'ai parlé la
langue française bien.?

lature, and bind a third, the executive (as well as the whole people), for all time. Nor has such a result always been acquiesced in. Declarations by colonial courts that laws were unconstitutional led to riots in New York and Rhode Island; and when the United States Supreme Court in 1832 declared a statute of Georgia to be unconstitutional, because it contravened a treaty of the United States with the Cherokee Indians, Andrew Jackson remarked — "John Marshall has made his decision; now let him enforce it"; and declined to interfere with the State's actions.

The fact seems to be that the judicial review of legislative action appealed to the people as a natural and convenient method of deciding apparent conflicts between the fundamental law as expressed in the written constitution, and the occasional law as expressed in acts of Congress or of state legislatures. We also have in our federal government a system which seems peculiarly to call for a single supreme umpire, to decide not only between the federal Constitution and Congress, but also between the federal Constitution and the constitutions and laws of the several States. What more natural than that the conflicts should be re-

ferred to an independent and presumably un-
prejudiced judiciary, with the Supreme Court
of the United States as final arbiter? And what
more natural than that conflicts between state
laws and state constitutions should, by analogy, be left to state courts?

Beginning with a jealousy of centralized
power in Congress on the part of States giving
up their independence to form a federal government, and followed in later generations with a
distrust of legislatures which did not prove to
be beyond the reach of corrupting influences,
we have always been more or less suspicious of
the legislative branch of the government. It
has not so promptly occurred to us that the
judicial branch might, though with the best of
intentions and perfect honesty of character,
fail to interpret correctly the spirit of our
civilization.

Historical research does not, however, carry
us far on our path. In the first place, it is
largely beside the mark, because it is not the
federal but the state courts that have been
particularly active in nullifying legislation; and
in the second place, it is largely academic,
because the court's power to declare a statute
void is now so generally recognized that noth-

ing short of a formal constitutional amendment can be expected to limit it. Such discussion may perhaps remind the courts that their authority is neither clear nor unquestioned; that they owe to the legislature at least a respectful attitude of presuming that every law is passed in the honest belief that it is authorized by the constitution; and that the constitution itself and not a former judicial decision is always the test by which each successive case should be decided.

If instead of concerning themselves wholly with the logical aspect of the question, the courts had originally considered its political bearing as well, it is probable that their attitude would from the first have been quite different. The constitutionality of a statute is fundamentally a political and not a legal question. The legislature and the executive are as much interested in its solution as the judiciary, and should be held equally responsible. There is no inevitable necessity that any one of the three departments of government should undertake the function of sole arbiter. In most countries the final decision rests with the legislature; it might conceivably be vested in the executive, especially after consultation with the judiciary.

In this country alone, largely through the failure of the judges themselves as well as the public to understand what was happening, has the function been allowed to vest in the judiciary. It is not surprising that so important a problem solved in so blind and haphazard a manner now returns to plague us.

The particular victims of judicial criticism have been laws intended to improve social conditions, and more particularly the conditions of wage-earners, in accordance with modern economic theories. The sweat-shop law, the bake-house law, and the workingmen's compensation act of New York are good examples; but for convenience of reference, they may all be fairly typified by the eight-hour law.

It is hardly necessary to point out that such laws are intended to change existing conditions. They are not mere regulations for future guidance, much less codifications of existing law or custom; they are positive, perhaps drastic, restrictions on methods and conditions under which business men are operating, and they are necessarily open to the criticism that they may injure some man's financial investment or restrict his activities. If a manufacturer is employing two hundred workmen in day and night shifts of twelve hours each, and the legislature enacts that the working day shall not exceed eight hours, the manufacturer may jump to the conclusion that his pay-roll will be increased by fifty per cent through the necessity of hiring a third shift, and that the extra expense will drive him into bankruptcy. Of course his conclusion may be, and probably is, quite far from the truth, in ignoring the increased capacity of his eight-hour laborers; but the argument remains, and can only be refuted by actual test. As the question is ordinarily carried into court by injunction before the effects of the new conditions can be demonstrated, the argument is certainly plausible.

These facts suggest the ground of legal challenge of such laws. The argument is that the statute, by depriving some person of liberty or property, violates the Fourteenth Amendment of the federal Constitution, which provides — "nor shall any State deprive any person of life, liberty, or property without due process of law." What constitutes "due process of law" is not fully defined; but the courts have always held that the enactment of a statute by the legislature is not in itself sufficient.

The Fourteenth Amendment has given rise

to an immense amount of litigation. An inspection of the cases in which it has been invoked justifies the conclusion that no statute affecting, however remotely, the habits or business methods of any person with money enough to bring a lawsuit is safe from attack on the ground of unconstitutionality. It has become the fashion in New York to argue that *every* statute is unconstitutional, and the courts of that State have become so technical [4] in their decisions that it is an open question whether any law there is valid until it has been sustained by the Court of Appeals. The method of attack, to take an eight-hour decision and a few recent examples at random, is this: —

(1) The New York eight-hour law contained a provision that municipal contracts must provide for eight hours' employment only, and that a contractor violating such provision could not recover his payment. It was argued, and the Court of Appeals, declaring this statute to be unconstitutional,[5] held, that as the contractor who brought suit had finished the work, he was entitled to payment, and to deny payment (because he had violated both contract and statute by working his men more than eight hours a day) would be to deprive

him of his property without due process of law!

(2) A statute required transient retailers advertising bankrupt stock to be licensed. The Court of Appeals held the law unconstitutional [6] because *every man "has the unqualified right to sell" his goods.* The Chief Judge went on to say that he believed that the statute was not passed in good faith to prevent fraud, but was intended to protect local trade from competition. This certainly is a good example of the attitude of open contempt and distrust which the courts are beginning to assume toward the legislature.

(3) The State of Illinois created a free employment agency which was forbidden to furnish lists of laborers in cases of strikes and lockouts. The Supreme Court held the law unconstitutional [7] because it *deprived both employer and workman of the "right of contract,"* which, said the Chief Justice, "is both a liberty and a property right."

Logically, if these arguments are valid in any case, — and their principle has repeatedly been sustained by the courts, both state and federal, — it becomes impossible to draw any line. Legislation would come to a standstill, and society would be crystallized into the condition in which it existed in 1868, when the Fourteenth Amendment took effect. The courts at once recognized this dilemma, and began to except from the operation of the rule a series of laws supposed to be enacted under a supreme governmental authority called the "police power." This no court has been willing to define except in the vaguest terms. It can best be understood by examples. For instance, legislation has been upheld regulating employment in mines, by forbidding the labor of women, children, and convicts, and limiting the day's work to eight hours;[8] providing for capital punishment by electricity;[9] granting an exclusive right to maintain a slaughter house within a city;[10] providing for the drainage of swamp lands;[11] regulating primary elections.[12]

Naturally courts have differed on the question whether any given law does or does not come within the "police power." One State will sustain a ten-hour law for women,[13] while another will declare it unconstitutional.[14] So it remains a gamble whether any particular law is valid or not; and the odds continue to be against it, because most States have a provision in their local constitutions identical with the

Fourteenth Amendment, and the statute has to pass the ordeal of the state court interpreting its own constitution as well as the United States Supreme Court interpreting the federal Constitution.

Moreover, the courts have created a virtual exception to the "police power" by inventing "the right to contract." This phrase was first sanctioned as recently as 1897. [15] Its far-reaching scope was quickly recognized, and it has been widely adopted by conservative courts; for it is diametrically opposed to the theory of the police power. If the individual has a "right" to contract, how can the legislature restrict such "right" without depriving him of liberty or property? It may be that he will contract to store dynamite in his front yard, or to send his ten-year-old son to work on night shifts in a coal mine; but has he not a "right to contract?"

The "right to contract" is generally called "a liberty." As such it is easy to see that it must give way to the best interests of the community. The restrictions necessarily imposed by society upon personal liberty are borne in upon the individual from his cradle. The distinction between liberty and license are taught, empirically at least, in the family and the grammar school. They are so fundamental, so obvious, and so necessary that no citizen of the United States, unless he be a lunatic or possibly an anarchist, contends for unrestricted liberty. The old cry, "Cannot I do what I will with mine own?" is heard less and less as the interests of the community as a whole are more and more widely recognized. If liberty were the only foundation for the "right to contract," it would need no argument to prove that the phrase has added nothing to constitutional law. But the word "right," with its implication of property, gives a most insidious twist to the phrase. It suggests to the conservative mind, accustomed to regard property as the foundation of society, an excuse for nullifying any law which impinges upon this "right."

Call it what you will, the "right to contract" effectually neutralizes the "police power," and leaves to chance the validity of any law attempting to regulate social or economic relations.

It does not seem to have occurred to the courts that there may be some subjects which the constitutions have not undertaken to regulate. It cannot be supposed that in 1788, nor even in 1868, the citizens of this country were in their constitution-building attempting to provide for or against an eight-hour law. The question simply was not present in their minds. What their attitude would have been on such a subject we can only surmise. But we have from the first adopted the spirit of liberal construction. We have permitted Congress to issue legal-tender notes, we have seen river and harbor improvements sustained, and we have welcomed the construction of the doubtful "general welfare" clause as authorizing practically unlimited functions of centralized government. It has never been seriously argued that the federal Constitution or its amendments were intended to crystallize society into the form it happened at the moment to have assumed, and to prevent all further growth and change of standards.

The truth of the matter seems to be that the great questions of social and economic relations now foremost among our political problems are within neither the letter nor the spirit of constitutional limitations, and are not properly cognizable by the courts at all. They should be excepted entirely from judicial review, instead of being tested by any theory of "police power." No matter how liberal a court may be, — and it is only fair to acknowledge that the United States Supreme Court has on the whole been more liberal than the courts of most of the States, — the difference in the point of view is vital. Under the "police-power" theory new legislation is presumptively invalid because it has taken somebody's property without due process of law. It can be sustained only as an exercise of an undefined power in the government to promote the morals, health, and safety of the people. Again, it leaves to the courts the function of deciding the precise boundaries of such legislation. For instance, five members of the court may think that a ten-hour law would be valid, while only four would go so far as an eight-hour law; and consequently the eight-hour law would be void for all time, though the court might undergo a change in membership the next week which would shift the majority over to the eight-hour view. Such questions ought not to be decided by any court. They are plainly the function of the legislature.

It is worth while to consider for a moment where the present system is leading us. As already pointed out, every decision by a court of last resort restricting legislation, in so far as it goes beyond the words of the constitution, is in effect *a constitutional amendment.* It establishes a precedent which the court assumes to follow in all future cases — perhaps a principle on which it will decide many different kinds of future cases. The invention of a theory like the "right to contract" is not mere "judicial legislation," an evil frequently discussed nowadays; it is much more — it is judicial constitution-making. A notorious example of such a mischief, though fortunately on a different subject, is the familiar Dartmouth College case, [16] where the United States Supreme Court, on reasoning that has never been understood, decided that a corporate franchise was an irrevocable contract. That decision came as a thunderbolt to the whole country, which had been proceeding on the true theory that the States had the same right to alter, amend, or repeal a franchise that they had to grant it. Its effect was to put forever beyond state control all the corporate charters then in existence. So when the court has decided that an eight-hour law is unconstitutional, it is immaterial that the subject-matter is not covered by any provision of the constitution, it is immaterial that the reasoning of the judges is unsound, it is immaterial that the public interests urgently demand such legislation, and that the great majority of the citizens are heartily in favor of the statute: the law is dead, and the situation is beyond all relief except by amendment of the constitution. The court has in an hour's time, and perhaps by a single vote, virtually amended the constitution. Is it just, or is it essential, that in order to correct this mischief the people should be relegated to the difficult and cumbersome method of formal constitutional amendment with all its effort, expense, and years of delay? [17]

CHAPTER II

The Present System

THE American theory of constitutional law is that a statute which does not conform to the commands and limitations of the constitution is utterly void — mere waste paper. No duties are imposed by it; no rights can be founded on it; it furnishes no protection to those who undertake to obey it; it can and must be pronounced invalid at the private instance of any person who claims to be aggrieved by it.

This theory is based on logic, with a fine disregard for political consequences; and it is a tribute to our political adaptability that it has, on the whole, wrought so little mischief. Stated as an original proposition, it is inconceivable that such a rule could ever have been accepted. Its inevitable result is to make every man his own judge of the validity of every statute until it has been construed by the court of last resort, and to impose on him the burden of guessing at his own peril whether or not it will be judicially approved. The mere statement of such a proposition would doubtless have been considered a *reductio ad absurdum* of the theory if it had been urged when the courts were first claiming the right of legislative review. Even now it ought to be sufficient to demonstrate a radical error in the judicial attitude.

The reason for the prevailing rule is not far to seek. It grew naturally, almost inevitably, out of a political philosophy wholly engaged in determining whether the courts ought to have *any* review of legislation — whether they could under any circumstances declare a law void. None of our early constitutions prescribed any method of testing the constitutionality of statutes, except for the barren experiment of a council of censors attempted in Pennsylvania, Vermont, and New York. In those States a council was created with the duty of supervising legislation and either reporting to the people instances of unconstitutionality, as in Pennsylvania and Vermont, or, as in New York, vetoing the statute, which might then be reënacted by a two-thirds vote of the legislature. None of the councils had power to give conclusive effect to its opinion,[1] and they were all abolished after short and ineffectual careers. Even in these States, and still earlier in the others, the question of judicial review was squarely presented to the courts.

(Confronted with the problem of a written constitution adopted by the people as a fundamental law and a statute enacted by the people's representatives in legislature in plain violation of the provisions of the constitution, the great majority of the judges felt that they could preserve the constitution intact only by disregarding the statute. They declared with substantial unanimity that such a law was "void." They seem, indeed, to have gone out of their way with rather undignified eagerness to announce this doctrine in cases where the conflict was by no means plain, or even where it was not involved at all;[2] but whatever the issue that called forth the discussion, they all confined their opinions to the purely logical proposition that what is contrary to the constitution cannot be law, and that a void statute is of no effect whatever. As a syllogism — which is as far as they undertook to test it — no fault can be found with this branch of their reasoning.) Tested by the practical requirements of a working government, or by common sense, the rule is pregnant with dangers from which the nation has been lucky to escape so lightly as it has. The seed of evil has nevertheless been sown, and it is time that we awoke to the need of sounder methods.

Practically the effect of deciding in a private controversy that a duly enacted statute has never been law is demoralizing to the legislatures, the courts, and the people. It gives the lawmakers a feeling of irresponsibility, since their work, if imperfect, is wholly undone; it puts the courts in a false position, because they are required to decide on insufficient data and prejudiced argument in a case that may be instigated and controlled by parties interested solely to annul the statute; it increases popular disrespect of authority by making every man his own judge of every new law. Politically it seems almost axiomatic that a statute duly enacted should be a law to all intents and purposes until it has been declared otherwise by proper authority. At the risk, then, of profoundly offending the conventional legal mind, I suggest that it may be worth while to abandon the prevailing logical but disastrously academic view, and see whether the simple expe-

dient of applying common sense to the problem
will not suggest some method of preserving
our constitutions without throwing us back on
a "judicial oligarchy," on the one hand, or an
unreflecting popular vote, on the other.

First let us examine somewhat more in detail the objections to the present system, which
grow out of the two features (1) that the law
is considered void *from the beginning*, and (2)
that the decision is made in litigation between
private parties.

Retroactive Effect. One obvious effect of our
theory of judicial review is to create a period
of doubt after the enactment of every important statute. Is it or is it not a law? Must we
conform to it at an inconvenience and expense
that will not be compensated if the statute
shall eventually be upset by the courts; or
shall we disregard it under penalty, perhaps,
of criminal prosecution if the law be sustained? From this dilemma we have as a
nation escaped with surprisingly slight damage. But that it is real, and may at any moment lead to serious consequences, has been
dramatically illustrated in at least one instance. In 1857 the New York legislature
passed an act reorganizing the police force of

the city of New York. The mayor and the
great majority of the police force, believing
the law to be unconstitutional, and supported
in that view by some of the ablest lawyers of
the day, refused to obey it. The new metropolitan board received the support of some
three hundred policemen, while the old municipal force retained eight hundred. Each side
undertook to dismiss those who refused alle-
giance and to fill its ranks with new men. Soon
two complete and hostile police forces were
in existence, and after frequent minor colli-
sions they met on the steps of the City Hall
in a fierce battle in which many were wounded
and several nearly killed. The disorder was
quelled only by the arrival of the militia and
the arrest of the mayor by the sheriff. During
the period of anarchy the city was wholly
demoralized; thieves grew rich and murderers
went unpunished.[3]

When order was finally reëstablished in the
city the mayor still had his own troubles to
meet. The injured metropolitan policemen
sued him and recovered judgments aggregat-
ing thirteen thousand dollars; so that in the
end the mayor was disgraced and ruined, fin-
ancially and politically, because he guessed

wrong on a question of law so doubtful that the Court of Appeals were divided in opinion on it, six to two.

The rule of the personal liability of a public officer for guessing wrong is the logical consequence of the doctrine of nullity, and prevails in the majority of States, though there are some exceptions.[4] For instance, a policeman arresting a drunkard under the direction of an act afterwards pronounced unconstitutional is liable in damages for false arrest.[5] So a statute in terms repealed by an unconstitutional law remains in force, and a person may be criminally prosecuted for not complying with it.[6] Purely private relations are everywhere conceded to be unaffected by "void" laws; so that individuals who built a bridge under legislative authorization afterwards annulled by the courts not only lost their investment, but had to turn over their toll receipts to their complaining rival.[7]

Many other examples might be added to show how the unfortunate citizen, whether in an official position or in private life, while seeking merely to obey the law, has committed a crime or incurred disastrous liability when it turns out that the legislative act was void;

but the situation after all is familiar. It is getting quite common for the administrative departments of the government practically to suspend operations under a new statute until it can be tested in the courts. A quick decision is sought by those most concerned, and a test case soon appears in court and is hurried through to the highest tribunal. This process somewhat relieves our difficulties; but it is unscientific, limited to statutes of great general importance, and fraught with dangers of its own.

Private Litigation. The courts have always prided themselves on the fact that their anulment of legislation is merely an incident of their decision of a case before them for adjudication. No method of reviewing legislation could possibly be less correct on principle, and less an object of pride; but passing for the moment the question of principle, let us look at some of the practical dangers.

For one thing a private lawsuit (including a criminal prosecution) is litigated according to the means of the parties and with the purpose, not of attaining the best possible review of constitutional principles, but of securing or resisting a judgment for money, for equitable relief, or for conviction of a crime. The parties may have very uneven opportunity for securing proper evidence, their attorneys may vary immensely in ability, and it often happens that while one side makes a fierce attack on a statute, the other submits but an indifferent defense, or is neutral, or possibly sympathetic on that issue. The human bias that even courts are not free from is also an element affecting the decision; and the old saying that "hard cases make bad law" makes no exception of constitutional cases.

Again, the litigation may not be brought in good faith. There was, for instance, evidence that the famous Ives case [8] was wholly under the control of the defendant railway, which was interested only in defeating the workingmen's compensation act. Intentional disobedience to a statute carrying criminal penalties is a favorite method of creating a test case; and such cases are not always free from the suspicion that they are brought in the domain of a prosecuting officer who is friendly to the defendant's view.

The rules of evidence applicable to private controversies may also keep out of the case all the facts which would inform the courts why the statute was enacted. The judges are thus thrown back on preconceived ideas, prejudices, and maxims, and may in their academic reasoning exhibit an almost pathetic ignorance of real conditions. In the New York sweatshop case,[9] for instance, the court certainly was not thinking of the noisome tenements of an overcrowded city when it said: "It cannot be perceived how the cigarmaker is to be improved in his health or his morals by forcing him from his home and its hallowed associations and beneficent influences, to ply his trade elsewhere." So in the woman's labor law case [10] the court cheerfully ignored all the teachings of biology in relation to the woman's physical capacity for manual labor when it said: "An adult female is not to be regarded as a ward of the State, or in any other light than the man is regarded, when the question relates to the business pursuit or calling. She is no more a ward of the State than is the man."

The legal practice on applications for injunction, also, is ill adapted to the decision of constitutional questions. It permits the parties to bring their case into court on affidavits, and thus paves the way for gross exaggerations on the part of an apprehensive plaintiff. It has frequently proved that the ill effects expected by merchants and manufacturers from statutes regulating prices and the hours and conditions of labor have not materialized. This is notably true of laws shortening the working days. Yet the case is presented and finally decided on sworn recitals of impending catastrophe which sound plausible enough, but really are mere imagination.

Finally, the interests most at stake — those of the public — are substantially ignored. Instead of being the real issue they are made a matter of incidental argument. It is the people of the State by whom and for whom the law is made — and yet the law is overthrown without giving them a hearing. Are we not entitled to ask whether such procedure is itself "due process of law"?

The Rights of the State

A law is an act of the supreme legislative body of a State — an expression of the will of the people through their representatives duly elected. It requires many formalities of procedure, imposed to prevent hasty or unconsidered action; and in spite of specific instances to the contrary, it fairly reflects the will of a

majority of the people. The political remedy
for unsatisfactory legislation is the ballot, by
which a new body of lawmakers may be elected
at frequent intervals and as a result of which
most laws that are disapproved may be
promptly repealed. It is true that money may
be extravagantly appropriated and spent before the next election, and that franchises may
be granted which create vested and permanent
rights; but laws are not often enacted in defi-
ance of an alert public opinion.

It is coming to be recognized more and more
clearly that direct responsibility to the people is the best assurance of competent government. This view has found its most emphatic
expression in municipal affairs, where for
many years there has been a steady increase
in the power of mayors at the expense of local
legislative bodies and subordinate officials;
and it is echoed in the growing authority of
our governors and presidents in legislation.
Any influence which tends to weaken responsibility or obscure it is fundamentally vicious.

Such an influence is the interference of our
courts in legislation. Not only does it divert
the attention of the public; but it has paved
the way for a hypocritical system of lawmak-

ing susceptible to great abuse. A legislature, reluctantly stirred to action by public opinion, frames a statute to meet the current demand by curbing the power of the political boss or correcting some corporate evil. After the first enthusiasm has begun to ebb and the first critical examination of the statute by the public has resulted in a favorable verdict, amendments begin to make their appearance, among which are one or more deliberately designed to make the whole statute unconstitutional. As the law will be *void from the beginning*, if unconstitutional at all, the threatened boss or corporation finds it easier and just as safe to rely on this insidious practice. Such procedure was openly charged in court when the New York franchise tax act was challenged as unconstitutional by the public service companies — though in that case their attorneys fortunately guessed wrong.

As no statute is certainly valid until approved by the judges, so the first step to check vicious legislation is to test it in court. Meanwhile the authors of it escape attention and perhaps secure a reëlection while the litigation is still under way. In any event, by the time a decision is reached the public interest has cooled, and if the law is pronounced unconstitutional, little further attention is paid to the legislators who voted for it. When a bad law is declared constitutional or a good law unconstitutional, the public is bewildered and impotently vents part of its wrath on the courts.

Through their increasing interference in legislation the courts have finally placed themselves in a false position and have succeeded in introducing into our legislative machinery a complication false in principle and vicious in effect. Some remedy must and undoubtedly will be applied at an early date. If no more efficient plan is devised than the somewhat clumsy "recall of judicial decisions," it seems altogether likely that either the power of judicial review will be taken away from the courts altogether or that all important legislation will be enacted in the guise of amendment to the constitution.[11] It has, therefore, become one of the most important political problems of the day to determine what review of legislation, if any, there should be.

A Remedy

Believing as I do that written constitutions are an extremely valuable feature of our government and should not be relegated to the level of statute law, I venture to suggest a method of reviewing legislation which involves no radical changes, and yet would, I believe, cure the defects of the existing procedure. My plan is based on a simple proposition, so obviously sound, as it seems to me, that it may be a commonplace maxim of political philosophy — and yet I do not recall running across it in any of the discussion over judicial review. It is this:

THE STATE IS AS MUCH CONCERNED IN THE ANNULMENT OF A LAW AS IN ITS ENACTMENT.

This means that no law should be declared void in litigation between private parties. It means that where a law is questioned, a direct proceeding should be brought against the State and the same consideration should be given as is required for its enactment. It means that the legislature and the persons instrumental in securing the legislation should have a hearing. And it would seem to be a corollary that the statute should be effective as law until annulled in such a proceeding.

Any political innovation is the more likely to succeed if it runs along familiar lines. My plan has at least the merit of proposing no

radical changes in existing methods. I believe
that the courts are competent to construe our
constitutions and that they are the best tribunals we could devise for that purpose. I
believe also that we have conceded to them so
long and so freely the power of judicial review
that we are as much bound to recognize their
prerogative as if it were expressly mentioned
in our constitutions. What we should seek to
attain is merely a different method of review
— one which does not relieve the legislature of
its responsibility for passing bad laws; one
which focuses deliberate, responsible, and un-
prejudiced attention upon constitutional principles when the issue is presented for review;
one which eliminates private interests and
gives the State representation at the hearing,
with the power to present both argument and
information. I strongly approve also of re-
quiring substantial unanimity on the part of the
judges. And finally I would suggest a time limit
within which the review may be applied for.

Although a formal constitutional amendment would doubtless be required to give it
effect, what I propose is little more than a
change of procedure. In brief and untechnical
language it is this:

Every statute duly enacted should have the force of law. If under its operation a party considers himself aggrieved, he may on notice to the attorney general apply to a court of general jurisdiction for a review of its constitutionality. If he can establish actual damage, the judge shall certify that fact to the highest court of the State which shall thereupon set an early date for a hearing on the validity of the statute. The State shall be represented, and notice shall be given to the members of the legislature which passed the act, and to the public. All persons interested shall have the right to intervene and argue, and untrammeled by technical rules of evidence, to present the reasons for the legislation. If the court shall, after such hearing, with substantial unanimity find the statute unconstitutional, it shall certify its decision to the secretary of state, and the statute shall, from that date only and to the extent indicated by the decision, cease to be law. The aggrieved plaintiff shall then be relegated to a court of claims to prove the amount of his injury and shall have judgment against the State for the damage he has suffered. All other persons who have meanwhile been aggrieved shall also be compensated in like manner; but no claim shall be made after ten years from the time when the statute takes effect.

The principal effect of this method of review is to place the responsibility where it belongs — on the State. The legislature, in the first place, will know when it enacts a statute that

that statute will be given effect for a limited time at least, and if it seriously disturbs vested interests, there will be a substantial bill of damages for the State to settle in the event of its annulment. The legislature, therefore, will be cautious in running the risk of unconstitutionality. It will, on the other hand, have the assurance of a fair hearing, an opportunity to present its evidence, and to tell the court why it believed the statute valid when it considered that question in its own debate.

The court will realize that it has a heavy responsibility and will quickly abandon the flippant tone that has crept into recent judicial utterances.[12] It will, on overthrowing the law, subject the State to a bill of damages of unknown weight. It will be annulling an existing and effectual law instead of destroying a mere phantom of words and leaving matters as if the statute never had been passed.

The court will, moreover, have no issue before it except the single question of unconstitutionality. Its attention will be not distracted by a complicated record, nor its sympathies stirred by a case of hardship. It will base its decision on actual facts instead of legal fictions. It will have less occasion to utter

obiter remarks about unconstitutional law.
If under those conditions it still finds a statute unconstitutional, its judgment will carry
much greater weight with the public.

The plaintiff will have to wait until he has
been damaged. No one will be allowed to cry
out until he has been hurt. The practice of
testing statutes by injunctions will vanish —
and in fact many intended suits will never be
brought, because actual experience under the
statute will demonstrate that there has been
no damage.

The plaintiff, again, will be pitted against
the State. He can neither "frame up" a case
nor create a misleading record, as is so easy
to do in the course of private litigation ham-
pered by rules of practice and evidence. On
important questions he will meet adversaries
equal in enthusiasm and ability. He will have
to fight fairly and in the open.

That this plan is illogical I freely concede,
nor am I concerned to defend it by a critique
of pure reason. We have tried the logical
method and have found that it works so badly
that if we stick to logic the result will probably to be vest the final decision either in the
legislature or in popular vote. That the plan

will expose the State to unlimited claims for damages is not necessarily an objection. A statute is, in the first place, the action of the State; its full effect ought to be considered before it is adopted, and when once the responsibility is assumed, the State ought to retain it. If there has been a mistake, it is the State and not its officers or private individuals who ought to pay the penalty. That the appellate court will have to give time to hearings and to decide on facts that are not provable under the common law rules of evidence, — though they may, of course, be produced under oath and cross-examination, — I regard as an unqualified advantage. It will emphasize the fact that legislation is at issue and will give a truer basis for decision than can possibly be attained from private litigation.

But will it work?

It is not possible to know in advance whether any political experiment will work. The best we can do, after stating our reasons for proposing the change, is to try to find an analogy and see if we can learn any lesson from it. The test that suggests itself is the attitude of the courts in that class of cases most nearly resembling constitutional questions as they would be presented under my plan. Is there now any class of cases where the constitutionality of the statute involved naturally impresses the court as a matter of grave concern to the State, where the controversy takes the form of an issue between the public and one disgruntled individual, and where vested rights and due process of law are unconsciously subordinated to the public welfare?

It occurred to me that the tax laws may furnish such an example. The responsibility for interfering with a system of taxation is obvious. No matter how the question may arise, the court can hardly escape the knowledge that to declare a tax law invalid may throw the state machinery into disastrous confusion. Nor is there much temptation for judges to tie the hands of the legislature so firmly that the State will be unable to obtain from whatever source it can find the revenue necessary to carry on the government.

With this idea in mind, and without any intimation in advance of what the results would be, I made an analysis of the constitutional decisions in the State of New York, which I submit for what it is worth. I selected

New York because it is commercially the most important State in the Union, because it is the theater of a vast amount of litigation, because its judicial decisions have served widely as precedents in other States, and because its courts have interfered with a free hand in legislation. Whether the New York figures are characteristic of other States I do not know, though it might be instructive to pursue the search further and get the complete story for the whole United States. The federal courts, however, are not on the same footing when construing state statutes; for they have no particular concern in the operation of the state governments, and hence have a much weaker feeling of responsibility in deciding their validity.

So many difficulties stand in the way of such an analysis as I have attempted that I at once disclaim any real accuracy in my figures. For instance, it is often a matter of opinion whether or not the constitutionality of a statute is necessarily involved in any given case — whether, though discussed, it is really decided. Still more is it matter of opinion how the statutes should be classified.[13] I venture to say that no two men would get exactly the same results from such an investigation as I have made.

I offer the following tabulation only as a picture of what exists. It has been made in a conscientious effort to discover the truth, and resembles, I trust, a photograph rather than an impressionist sketch.

	Statutes sustained	Statutes overruled	Total statutes construed	Percentage overruled
Administrative.......	156	48	204	23.5
Elections............	12	8	20	40.0
Highways and Water-ways..............	82	32	114	28.0
Judiciary, Legislative, and Military.......	145	59	204	29.0
Local and Private....	39	25	64	39.0
Public Service........	77	25	102	24.5
Social and Economic..	185	69	254	27.0
Taxes and Assessments	84	19	103	18.0
Total...........	780	285	1065	27.0
Taxes...........	56	4	60	7.0
Assessments......	28	15	43	35.0

The figures are suggestive in more aspects than one; but passing the startling fact that over one quarter of all the statutes challenged have been overruled, I call attention only to this: that the percentage of overruled statutes relating to "Taxes and Assessments" is the lowest of any group, and well below the average, although the number of statutes construed is greater than those in several other groups. But there is an important distinction between a tax and an assessment; and if we analyze our figures still further we find the percentage of "Tax" laws overruled falling to 7, as against an average of 27 and a maximum of 40. "Assessments" alone with a percentage of 35, then approximate the 39 per cent of "Local and Private" statutes, to which they are rather closely related.

With all the explanation that may be made, I do not believe that these figures are accidental. Neither can they be accounted for as showing exceptional care and wisdom on the part of the legislature — the variations are too great for that. If they show anything, they show a marked tendency on the part of the judiciary to "go slow" when they feel genuine responsibility without economic or political prejudice.

If all constitutional questions could be brought before them in the same solemn, dispassionate way, it seems reasonable to expect from them a similar attitude toward all legislation. If that result were attained, it would be highly satisfactory. Until our standards of legislation have considerably improved, we shall not have much cause for complaint if no more than seven per cent of the statutes doubtful enough to be seriously challenged are held unconstitutional.

CHAPTER III

ANNULMENT OF LEGISLATION BY THE SUPREME COURT

THE United States Supreme Court assumes to decide the constitutionality of acts of Congress, and its decisions are accepted as final. What is the origin of this important power?

The question, it may be argued, is purely academic. The authority of the Supreme Court is so well recognized that its source is a matter of no importance. While that argument is largely true, it is also true that the judicial review of legislation is so far from satisfactory in its results that changes of method are unquestionably impending,[1] and history can assist us in attaining a proper perspective for the study of the political problem that confronts us to-day. The historical study is interesting also in showing that our forefathers in their discussions by no means adopted the viewpoint of most of the modern writers — of assuming that whenever a law is declared unconstitutional, the court is always right and is performing a public service in so deciding. And more important still, it suggests the true theory, not clearly formulated then and wholly overlooked in recent discussion, that *constitutionality is a political and not a legal question.*

Investigation in this field has already been pursued by several able writers. In 1911 [2] appeared several magazine articles, contending on historical grounds that the action of the courts was substantially "usurpation"; while in 1912 [3] were published two books, which, on the basis of careful and scholarly research, reached an opposite conclusion. In view of the thoroughness with which the ground has been covered, it may be rash to enter the lists with further argument; yet the interest of the topic justifies the effort to throw more light on it. Several phases of the subject tempt discussion, but for the purposes of a single paper I must confine myself strictly to an attempt to answer the one question — Did our forefathers who adopted the Constitution intend to give the federal Supreme Court the power conclusively to determine the constitutionality of acts of Congress?

In my judgment they did not.

As I reach this conclusion upon much the same evidence as is cited by Professor Beard in his interesting study, it is necessary to define the question with some care, and to point out specifically the differences of opinion between us. In the first place, Professor Beard discusses primarily the attitude of the *makers* of the Constitution (p. 1), while I am concerned primarily with those who *adopted* it. But I am also inclined to question his demonstration of the *intent* of the makers, especially his contention that seventeen of them "*declared*, directly or indirectly, *for judicial control*" (p. 17), and that "twenty-five members of the convention *favored* or at least accepted *some form of judicial control*" (p. 51).

If we could discover the intent of the several conventions that ratified the Constitution, we should have a guide to the meaning that historically ought to be attached to it; and if we found that a majority of all the conventions understood the article relating to the judiciary to the same effect, and intended the same significance to be attached to their respective actions, — whether ratifying without qualification, or ratifying and at the same time urging amendment, or finally, rejecting, — we should have the most cogent argument possible on its proper interpretation. Unfortunately it is impossible to determine the intent of the conventions with any such exactness, partly because there is no known record of the debates in some of them, and partly because the question was not presented in such a way as to get any clear and unequivocal answer.

In trying to discover the intent of our forefathers who adopted the Constitution, I shall begin with the opinions of the members of the constitutional convention, reviewing the ground covered by Professor Beard; I shall then discuss the debates and proceedings of the several ratifying conventions, in the light of contemporary discussion, touching on the ground covered by Professor McLaughlin; and finally I shall analyze the judiciary act of 1789, as a contemporary interpretation by men fresh from the controversy in which most of them had engaged. Beyond that I do not find much significance in either legal or political action. It seems to me that the Virginia and Kentucky Resolutions and their reception indicate the politics of the moment, rather than any fixed philosophical views about the method of determining the constitutionality of laws; [4] and that Chief Justice Marshall's opinion in the case of *Marbury* v. *Madison* [5] was a shrewd political manifesto, rather than a logical foundation for the decision of that highly technical case.

A brief summary of my argument will make my position clearer. Conceding that the theory of a judiciary assuming to declare statutes to be unconstitutional and void was in accord with the political philosophy of the period, was brought to the attention of the constitution-makers as practicable, and was favored by some of the most influential members of the convention as a deliberate policy — yet the evidence that I have been able to gather persuades me that there was in the convention itself great difference of opinion as to the best policy to be adopted; that the question was intentionally left open; that upon the submission of the Constitution for ratification a vigorous objection to the power of the federal judiciary was expressed, especially in the most important States; that the jealousy of federal power crystallized into the Tenth Amendment, one of the effects of which was intended to be, and logically was, to deprive the federal courts of the power of constitutional review; and that this limitation was recognized and applied in the judiciary act of 1789, *by leaving this power to the States.* If my reading of the evidence is correct, it follows that the people of the original States did not intend to give the federal Supreme Court the power of annulling acts of Congress on the ground of unconstitutionality.

The Intent of the Constitutional Convention

Accepting Professor Beard's list of twenty-five as representing the active and influential members of the constitutional convention, let us first analyze his division of them into those "who directly or indirectly supported the doctrine of judicial control" and those who did not regard judicial control as "a normal judicial function."

I do not intend to repeat the evidence he has so fully and fairly collated from Farrand, Elliot, and other sources; but it will make the argument clearer to reproduce his list, with the names in italics, as printed by him, to indicate the seventeen who, as he concludes, "declared, directly or indirectly, for judicial control." His list is as follows (p. 17):

Blair	*Johnson*	Pinckney, Chas.
Butler	*King*	Pinckney, C. C.
Dayton	*Madison*	*Randolph*
Dickinson	*Martin, L.*	Rutledge
Ellsworth	*Mason*	Sherman
Franklin	*Morris, G.*	*Washington*
Gerry	*Morris, R.*	*Williamson*
Gorham	*Paterson*	Wilson
Hamilton		

For purposes of comparison I repeat the
list, leaving in italics those who from first to
last *favored* judicial control, putting in small
capitals those who *disapproved*, and leaving
in lower case the doubtful and non-committal
ones. I hasten to add that my list, like Professor Beard's, is only tentative; and I may
express also my doubt of the possibility of
ever reaching a final conclusion, not only because the evidence is slight, but also because
of the probability that some of those who spoke
or wrote on the subject were not altogether
clear in their own minds. The course of the
debate in which the speaker was engaged and
the politics of the moment seem to have influenced not a few remarks on this subject; and
it is probable that the views of some of our
forefathers were quite unsettled. With these
qualifications, and with the further important distinction that it is the final view of

each member, as shown upon or immediately after the ratification by his State (between December, 1787, and October, 1789) that I seek to emphasize, not his opinion in the convention, my revision is as follows:

Blair	JOHNSON	PINCKNEY, CHAS.
Butler	*King*	Pinckney, C. C.
Dayton	MADISON	Randolph
Dickinson	MARTIN, L.	Rutledge
ELLSWORTH	*Mason*	Sherman
Franklin	*Morris, G.*	WASHINGTON
Gerry	MORRIS, R.	*Williamson*
Gorham	PATERSON	*Wilson*
Hamilton		

JOHN DICKINSON, of Delaware, expressly declared himself in the convention as opposed to the "power of the judges to set aside the law," but "at a loss what expedient to substitute"; nevertheless he is included by Professor Beard as one of the seventeen because of an argument in favor of the ratification of the Constitution, written in 1788, in which he accepts the theory of judicial review.[6] But in the same paper Dickinson adds:[7] "Constitutional properties are only, as has been observed at the beginning of this letter, parts in the organization of the contributed rights. As long as those parts preserve the orders assigned to them respectively by the constitution, they may so far be said to be balanced; but, when one part, without being sufficiently checked by the rest, abuses its power to the manifest danger of public happiness, or when the several parts abuse their respective power so as to involve the commonwealth in like peril, *the people* must restore things to that order from which their functionaries have departed" (italics in original).

In another paper in the same series he inquires: [8]

"What bodies are there in Britain, vested with such capacities for inquiring into, checking and regulating the conduct of national affairs, as our sovereign states?"

It would seem from these remarks that while Dickinson appreciated the possibility of judicial review, he contemplated also direct action by the people and intervention by the States. Whether he at any time *approved* of the court's exercise of the function of annulling legislation seems to me more than doubtful in view of his original objection; but neither am I convinced that he *disapproved*. I class him, therefore, as doubtful.

OLIVER ELLSWORTH, of Connecticut, did not express himself in the federal convention, but in the state convention in January, 1788, he clearly and tersely voiced the doctrine of judicial control as an argument in favor of the Constitution.[9] This, it will be observed, was before the debates in Massachusetts, the Carolinas, Virginia, and New York had disclosed the strength of the Anti-Federalist sentiment. In March, 1789, Ellsworth took his seat in Congress as Senator from Connecticut, and was at once appointed chairman of the judiciary committee. He had framed the judiciary bill himself and was active both in committee and on the floor of the Senate, as appears from Senator Maclay's Journal, in preserving it in a form satisfactory to himself. As sponsor for the bill from its introduction to its final passage, he is fully committed to its principle of reserving the judicial review of legislation to the state courts; and I, therefore, class him as *disapproving* federal judicial control.

ELBRIDGE GERRY, of Massachusetts, seems on the whole to have accepted the theory of judicial review. His speeches in the federal convention in 1787 and in the House of Representatives in 1789 are quoted fully by Professor Beard, and need not be repeated. Nevertheless it is worthy of comment that he refused to sign the Constitution, assigning as one of his reasons: [10] "My principal objections to the plan are . . . that the judicial department will be oppressive."

He campaigned actively against the ratification of the Constitution, publishing in 1788 "Observations on the New Constitution; By a Columbian Patriot," in which he expressed his dread of the judiciary more fully as follows: [11]

"But I leave the field of general censure on the secrecy of its birth, the rapidity of its growth, and the fatal consequences of suffering it to live to the age of maturity, and will particularize some of the most weighty objections to its passing through this continent in a gigantic size. . . .

"3. There are no well defined limits of the Judiciary Powers; they seem to be left as a boundless ocean, that has broken over the chart of the Supreme Lawgiver, '*thus far shalt thou go and no further*,' and as they cannot be comprehended by the clearest capacity, or the most sagacious mind, it would be an Herculean labour to attempt to describe the dangers with which they are replete."

If he was sincere in this argument, it is difficult to believe that he *approved* of giving to the Supreme Court the highest power imaginable — that of annulling an act of Congress; — yet his speeches the following year on the President's power of removal show none of the apprehension he expressed during the struggle for ratification.[12]

JAMES MADISON, of Virginia. Madison's views are discussed so fully and with such liberal quotations by Professor Beard that I have nothing new to add. I can only say that the extracts he gives are convincing to my mind that Madison strongly disapproved the theory that the federal judges should have power conclusively to determine the constitutionality of acts of Congress. I may mention particularly the following: [13]

"In the state constitutions and indeed in the federal one also, no provision is made for the case of a disagreement in expounding them [the laws], and as the courts are generally the last making the decision, it results to them, by refusing or not refusing to execute a law, to stamp it with its final character. This makes the judiciary department paramount in fact to the legislature, which was never intended and can never be proper."

Madison's earnest and repeated efforts to provide for a council of revision seem to me to show a consistent desire to avoid leaving to the court any question of annulment of legislation. He also took the lead in the House of Representatives in 1789 in securing the passage of the first ten amendments, which, as I argue, remove from the Supreme Court to the States the authority to annul acts of Congress.

LUTHER MARTIN, of Maryland, refused to sign the Constitution and fought actively against its ratification. He delivered to the legislature of Maryland, November 29, 1787, an address [14] which was one of the most complete and able arguments made by any of the Anti-Federalists. He argues, *as a reason for rejecting the Constitution:*

"Whether, therefore, any laws or regulations of the congress, or any acts of its President or other officers, are contrary to or not warranted by the Constitution, rests only with the judges, who are appointed by Congress, to determine; by whose determination every State must be bound."

His view is indicated more fully in his "Reply to the Landholder," dated March

19, 1788,[15] where he describes his effort in the federal convention to have all questions of the constitutionality of laws decided by the state courts.

"When this clause ['that the legislative acts of the United States . . . shall be the supreme law of the respective States . . . anything in the respective laws of the individual States to the contrary notwithstanding'] was introduced, it was not established that inferior continental courts should be appointed for trial of all questions arising on treaties and on the laws of the general government, and it was my wish and hope that every question of that kind would have been determined in the first instance in the courts of the respective states; had this been the case, the propriety and necessity that treaties duly ratified, and the laws of the general government, should be binding on the state judiciaries, *which were to decide upon them*, must be evident to every capacity, while at the same time, if such treaties or laws were inconsistent with our constitution and bill of rights, the judiciaries of this state would be bound to reject the first and abide by the last, since in the form I introduced the clause, notwithstanding treaties and the laws of the general government were intended to be superior to the laws of our State government, where they should be opposed to each other, yet that they were not proposed nor meant to be superior to our constitution and bill of rights."

This scheme of Martin's would have made the state constitutions superior to the federal laws, and it is the clash between the two that he is discussing; but his proposal, especially in the absence of inferior federal courts, would have left questions of the validity of federal laws, under the federal Constitution also, to the determination of state courts, as appears from the words I have italicized.

GEORGE MASON, of Virginia, is counted as favoring judicial control because of a speech in the Virginia convention in June, 1788, in which he said:

"When this matter comes before the federal judiciary, they must determine according to this constitution. . . . As an express power is given to the federal court to take cognizance of such controversies, and to declare null all *ex post facto* laws, I think gentlemen must see there is danger, and that it ought to be guarded against." [16]

Mason, like Gerry, refused to sign the Constitution and argued vigorously against its ratification. In fact, the speech above quoted was delivered not in favor of the Constitution, but in opposition to it. With the exception of these remarks, his whole attitude seems adverse to vesting such power in the judiciary. In the constitutional convention he favored Madison's plan for a council of revision; in October, 1787, he wrote Washington [17] objecting to the prohibition against *ex post facto* laws because "there never was, nor can be, a legislature, but must and will make such laws, when necessity and the public safety require them, which will hereafter be a breach of all the constitutions in the union, and *afford precedents for other innovations*" — evidently not then relying on the courts to check such legislation; and he is credited with the authorship of the Virginia amendments intended to limit the power of the federal judiciary.[18]

His approval of the theory of judicial control seems on the whole to rest on a slender foundation.

WILLIAM PATERSON, of New Jersey. On the strength of a charge to the jury in 1795 delivered by Paterson as circuit judge in the case of *Van Horne's Lessee* v. *Dorrance*,

2 Dallas, 304, he is listed by Professor Beard among the seventeen. The remarks quoted are broad enough to justify this classification, but they lose their significance when the circumstances of the case are considered. That case was brought in the federal court, apparently as a controversy between citizens of different States, and the question was whether a statute of Pennsylvania was valid under the Pennsylvania constitution. Neither the Constitution of the United States nor any act of Congress was relied on by either party; nor did it appear that the Pennsylvania statute had ever been construed by the state court. Hence there can be no positive inference that Paterson believed that the federal Supreme Court should have the power conclusively to determine the constitutionality of acts of Congress.

On the other hand, he was in 1789 a member of the Senate committee which framed the judiciary bill, and as Senator from New Jersey he voted for it. If, as I shall endeavor to show, this statute placed the authority to annul unconstitutional federal statutes exclusively in the States, then Paterson must be counted as disapproving the exercise of that power by the federal courts.

CHARLES PINCKNEY, of South Carolina. Charles Pinckney did not express himself in the federal convention, but in 1799 he wrote: [19]

"On no subject am I more convinced, than that it is an unsafe and dangerous doctrine in a republic, ever to suppose that a judge ought to possess the right of questioning or deciding upon the constitutionality of treaties, laws, or any act of the legislature. It is placing the opinion of an individual, or of two or three, above that of both branches of Congress, a doctrine which is not warranted by the constitution, and will not, I hope, long have any advocates in this country."

EDMUND RANDOLPH, of Virginia, refused to sign the Constitution. He set forth his reasons in a long letter to the speaker of the house of delegates in which he writes: [20]

"I should now conclude this letter, which is already too long, were it not incumbent on me, from having contended for amendments, to set forth the particulars, which I conceive to require correction. . . . 8. In limiting and defining the judicial power."

As a member of the Virginia convention, he argued: [21]

"Can congress go beyond the bounds pre-

scribed in the Constitution? Has congress a
power to say that she [Virginia] shall pay fifteen
parts out of sixty-five parts [of a direct tax]?
Were they to assume such a power it would
be a usurpation so glaring, that rebellion would
be the immediate consequence."

By December, 1790, however, he seems to
have lost his dread of the federal judiciary.
At that date he reported to Congress a criticism of the judiciary act of 1789 and a draft
statute which would have immensely increased
the jurisdiction of the federal courts. An analysis of the proposed law would be too long and
too technical for this paper, but it appears to
authorize both the Circuit Courts and the
Supreme Court to review the decisions of
state courts on any federal question; and it is
significant that it provides that both District
and Circuit Courts "shall have original jurisdiction in all cases of law and equity arising
under the Constitution of the United States,
the laws of the United States, and treaties."
In commenting on the proposed statute, Randolph recognizes the right of state courts to
invalidate acts of Congress as unconstitutional,
though even in a rather lengthy discussion of
the subject he does not hint that federal courts

have such right. His argument, however, is based on the contingency of the statute being actually constitutional and the decision of the state court merely "refractory," [22] and does not preclude the theory of federal judicial review.

If this report and his failure to argue in the Heyburn case,[23] in 1792, that the judges had no power to declare the law unconstitutional, indicate a change of heart because he had been appointed attorney general and was anxious for an extension of power of the machine of which he had become part, then his opinion ought to be cited from the earlier date; but on the evidence before me, that fact must remain a matter of surmise, and therefore, I classify him as doubtful.

WILLIAM JOHNSON, of Connecticut, ROBERT MORRIS, of Pennsylvania, and GEORGE WASHINGTON. For precisely the reason that Professor Beard concludes that these three members "understood and indorsed the doctrine" of judicial review, I infer that while they may well have understood it, they not only did not indorse it, but actually disapproved it. The only evidence is the support of the judiciary act of 1789 by Johnson and

Morris with their votes in the Senate and by Washington with his signature as President.

JOHN BLAIR, of Virginia, ALEXANDER HAMILTON, of New York, RUFUS KING, of Massachusetts, GOUVERNEUR MORRIS, of Pennsylvania, HUGH WILLIAMSON, of North Carolina, and JAMES WILSON, of Pennsylvania, committed themselves to approval of judicial control.[24] Gerry should be included with this group on the basis of his more frequent and more specific utterances, and Mason may be added for similar reasons.

Taking now the preliminary census of the attitude of the twenty-five active and influential members of the constitutional convention, as shown from 1787 to 1789, we find: *Favoring* judicial control by the Supreme Court, Blair, Gerry, Hamilton, King, Mason, G. Morris, Williamson and Wilson, 8; *disapproving* of such control, Ellsworth, Johnson, Madison, L. Martin, R. Morris, Paterson, Chas. Pinckney and Washington, 8; *doubtful or noncommittal*, Butler, Dayton, Dickinson, Franklin, Gorham, C. C. Pinckney, Randolph, Rutledge and Sherman,[25] 9.

Turning to the less important members, my view of the judiciary act of 1789 leads me to suggest further changes in Professor Beard's grouping.

William Few, of Georgia, George Read, of Delaware, and Caleb Strong, of Massachusetts, all voted for the statute; in addition, Few and Strong were members of the judiciary committee of the Senate, which introduced and supported the bill. Their action in so doing places them, for reasons just stated, in the list of those who disapproved federal judicial review. It may also be remarked that Strong failed to sign the Constitution.

Richard Bassett, of Delaware, was also a member of the Senate judiciary committee and voted for the statute, thus indicating in 1789 his disapproval of federal judicial review. His memorial to Congress in 1802, suggesting that his right to compensation as a judge appointed under the act of February 13, 1801, (repealed March 8, 1802) be submitted to judicial decision, is cited as evidence of the contrary attitude thirteen years later. But is it? Is there not a suggestion of shrewd personal politics in the attempt to have the Republican legislation subjected in some extra-judicial proceeding to the examination and decision of the Federalist bench? And in any case, is not

Bassett's proposal evidence rather of a continued *disapproval* of federal judicial review? His suggestion is that the act of 1802 is unconstitutional and that *Congress* take steps to have it so declared. That is the very opposite of judicial control; it is decision by the legislature itself through machinery of its own invention. Any decision by the judiciary was to be merely on the invitation of the legislature. If Bassett believed that the judiciary independently had the conclusive determination, why did he not get his question into court in a legally initiated action or proceeding, as he might have done in a dozen different ways?

Robert Yates, of New York, withdrew from the federal convention, and argued and voted against the Constitution when it came up for ratification. His views on judicial control are fully and ably expressed in the "Brutus" letters, referred to again below. That he regarded it as a logical but altogether undesirable deduction, appears from the whole tenor of his argument, summed up in Letter XV [26] as follows:

"I said in my last number, that the supreme court under this constitution would be exalted above all other powers in the government, and subject to no control. The business of this paper will be to illustrate this, and to shew the danger that will result from it. . . .

"There is no control above them that can either correct their errors or control their decisions. . . . "

George Wythe, of Virginia, Pierce Butler, of South Carolina, and John Langdon, of New Hampshire. The evidence as to all three of these members seems to me too slight to justify their classification. Wythe did not sign the Constitution; and in the Virginia convention he was chairman of a committee on amendments, which reported a set of proposals for the limitation of the federal judiciary to a supreme court, with little except appellate jurisdiction, and inferior courts of *admiralty only*. His opinion six years earlier in a case involving only a state law must be considered in the light of his action on the Constitution itself. As to Butler and Langdon, they may have had a score of reasons for voting against the judiciary act; I do not feel that such action is indicative of a view either in favor of or against judicial control.

As to William Livingston, of New Jersey, also, the evidence is very meagre. Professor

Beard infers that from his connection with the
early and unreported case of *Holmes* v. *Walton*,
deciding a New Jersey statute to be unconstitutional and void (1780), he shows an understanding and approval of the doctrine of judicial review; and Mr. Austin Scott, discussing
that case in the *American Historical Review*,[27]
writes that "Livingston, as governor . . . had
shared in the legislative acquiescence in the
decision of the court." In fact the only "acquiescence," was the passage of another act
on the same subject, in 1779, *before* the court
had made its decision. The act of 1779 was,
however, framed to meet the arguments made
on constitutional grounds, and perhaps gives
color enough to Mr. Scott's conclusion to justify the classification of Livingston among
those who approved of judicial control, in the
absence of evidence to the contrary.

Abraham Baldwin, of Georgia, and David
Brearly, of New Jersey, also appear to have
favored judicial control. The evidence is a
quotation from Baldwin,[28] and Brearly's par-
ticipation as chief justice in the decision of
Holmes v. *Walton*.

Gunning Bedford, of Delaware, John F.
Mercer, of Maryland, and Richard Spaight, of

North Carolina,[29] showed by their speeches that they were opposed to judicial control.

The final count thus adds to those *in favor* of judicial control the names of Baldwin, Brearly and Livingston, 3, making a total of 11; to those *against* judicial control it adds Bassett, Bedford, Few, Mercer, Read, Spaight, Strong and Yates, 8, making a total of 16; and to the *doubtful* it adds Butler, Langdon and Wythe, 3, making a total of 12. If we add to the third group the names of those who signed the Constitution but have not been mentioned thus far in the discussion, we shall fairly have disposed, as best we can, of all members of the convention entitled to consideration in ascertaining the opinions of the framers. This silent and not particularly influential group is as follows: William Blount, of North Carolina; Jacob Broom, of Delaware; Daniel Carroll, of Maryland; George Clymer and Thomas Fitzsimons, of Pennsylvania; Nicholas Gilman, of New Hampshire; Jared Ingersoll, of Pennsylvania; Daniel S. Jenifer and James McHenry, of Maryland; and Thomas Mifflin, of Pennsylvania, 10; making the total for the *doubtful and non-committal* members, 22.

This uncertain and tentative grouping shows

11 for and 16 against judicial control out of
48 members who either signed the Constitution or took a fairly active part in its making
— a reasonably even division of opinion when
we consider the meagreness of the evidence
on which we are obliged to rely. It accounts
for the very illuminating letter written by
Gouverneur Morris, the draftsman of the final
version of the Constitution, in 1814, in which
he says [30] (italics mine):

"MY DEAR SIR, — What can a history of
the Constitution avail towards interpreting
its provisions? This must be done by com-
paring the plain import of the words with the
general tenor and object of the instrument.
That instrument was written by the fingers
which write this letter. Having rejected re-
dundant and equivocal terms, I believed it to
be as clear as our language would permit; ex-
cepting, nevertheless, a part of what relates
to the judiciary. On that subject, *conflicting
opinions had been maintained with so much
professional astuteness*, that it became necessary
to select phrases which, expressing my own
notions, would not alarm others nor shock their
self-love; and to the best of my recollection, this
was the only part that passed without cavil."

It would be difficult to understand Morris's allusion to "conflicting opinions," if on the important subject of judicial review of legislation the members had been practically unanimous — twenty-five (including all the active ones who expressed themselves) against five (according to Professor Beard's final list — or three, if we exclude Butler and Langdon); but with such an even split in opinion as is indicated by my list, it is easy to understand that tact and skill in selecting phrases became indispensable.

Is it not the legitimate inference that the power of judicial control was neither overlooked, nor attempted to be slipped in by indirect or ambiguous phrases, but that it was intentionally omitted? [31]

The Intent of the Ratifying Conventions

To get a correct perspective for interpreting the action of the people in ratifying the Constitution, we must keep in mind a few familiar facts of political history.

In 1787 the thirteen original States, having achieved their independence, were banded together in a loose confederation. Although the Articles of Confederation had proved totally inadequate to provide an efficient central government, the Philadelphia convention was organized merely to *revise* those articles, and the authority of some of its members was in terms limited to such action.[32] The people as a whole were by no means prepared for the creation of a vigorous central government. Apart from local pride and mutual jealousy, questions of unequal practical advantage made the favorable reception of the new plan a matter of the greatest uncertainty. The smaller States could be counted upon to support a centralized government which would remove restrictions on interstate trade; but the powerful States of Virginia, Massachusetts, Pennsylvania and New York were offered less obvious advantages, and yet without the support of all of them the new Union could hardly be expected to be a success. Moreover the Constitution was offered for ratification, to be accepted or rejected as a whole; and there was little occasion for academic discussion of detail. The big question was whether "the grinding necessity" of the political situation was stern enough to extort a consent from a reluctant people.[33]

The chief topic of debate was almost of

necessity the question of state sovereignty. What powers of government were the States surrendering, and what were they retaining? The first three words of the preamble — "We the people" — provoked as much discussion as any whole article in the Constitution itself; and in one form or another the argument over that phrase continued until it was settled by the Civil War. The absence of any bill of rights in favor of either the people or the States caused a storm of criticism which was met only by a general understanding that the principles involved would be incorporated promptly into the Constitution by amendment.

Other questions which were fully argued were the basis of representation in the House of Representatives, the frequency of elections, the power of taxation and especially the right to levy direct taxes, the control over federal elections, the method of impeachment, the making of treaties, the power of the executive, the creation of a federal judiciary, the separation or confusion of function among the three branches of government, the debt of the Confederation, and slavery — some of them matters which have proved to be of little importance, but others going to the foundation of our sys-

tem of government. Much alarm was caused
by the vague language of the Constitution,
which, it was argued, would permit the central government to absorb all the functions of
the state governments. With these questions
at issue, the method of testing and checking
violations of the instrument itself could hardly
rank higher than a secondary topic. When it
was broached, it was often discussed in the
most general terms. The same factors were
often spoken of as checks upon the abuse of
any authority, whether legislative or executive,
namely, frequent elections, impeachment, and
amendment of the Constitution.

Viewed in this broad aspect, it would be
surprising to find any clear expression of popular opinion on a single technical issue not presented by any language in the document under
consideration. Nevertheless the issue was not
wholly overlooked, and if all the debates had
been preserved in full, it is probable that we
should find considerable argument on the subject. Without pretending to have made an
exhaustive search, I submit what I have been
able to gather, arranging the material by States
in the order of their ratification.

DELAWARE ratified the Constitution on

December 6, 1787, by a unanimous vote and without debate.

PENNSYLVANIA followed December 12, 1787, after three weeks of animated debate, by a vote of 46 to 23. The speeches of the Federalists led by James Wilson and Thomas McKean have been preserved, and there can be no doubt that the principle of judicial control was fully expounded by them and was accepted by the convention. On November 24, McKean presented the theory distinctly in a speech summarized by Wilson as follows: [34]

"In order to secure Liberty and the Constitution, it is absolutely necessary that the legislature should be restrained.

"It may be restrained in several ways:

"1. By the judges deciding agst the legislature in favor of the Constn."

The Anti-Federalists were led by John Smilie, Robert Whitehill and William Findley. On the 28th of November, Smilie and Whitehill both discussed the question, Smilie beginning with the following remarks: [35]

"So loosely, so inaccurately are the powers which are enumerated in this Constitution defined, that it will be impossible, without a test of that kind [bill of rights], to ascertain the limits of authority, and to declare when government has degenerated into oppression. In that event the contest will be between the people and the rulers: 'You have exceeded the powers of your office, you have oppressed us,' will be the language of the suffering citizen. The answer of the government will be short — 'We have not exceeded our power; you have no test by which you can prove it.' Hence, Sir, it will be impracticable to stop the progress of tyranny, for there will be no check but the people, and their exertions must be futile and uncertain.''

Whitehill said:

"Besides the powers enumerated, we find in this Constitution an authority is given to make all laws that are necessary to carry it effectually into operation, and what laws are necessary is a consideration left for congress to decide.''

And Smilie continued:

"Those very men who raise and appropriate the taxes are the only judges of what shall be deemed the general welfare and common defence of the national government.''

Wilson argued the point elaborately on December 1, and referred to it again answering unreported speeches of Smilie and Whitehill on December 4 and 7. In the first of these addresses he said: [36]

"It is therefore proper to have efficient restraints upon the legislative body. These restraints arise from different sources. I will mention some of them. In this Constitution they will be produced, in a very considerable degree, by a *division of the power* in the legislative body itself. Under this system, they may arise likewise from the interference of those officers who will be introduced into the executive and judicial departments. They may spring also from another source — the election by the people; and finally, under this Constitution, they may proceed from the great and last resort — from the *people* themselves. I say, under this Constitution, the legislature may be restrained, and kept within its prescribed bounds, by the interposition of the judicial department. This I hope, sir, to explain clearly and satisfactorily. I had occasion, on a former day, to state that the power of the Constitution was paramount to the power of the legislature acting under that Constitution; for it is possible that the legislature, when acting in that capacity, may transgress the bounds assigned to it, and an act may pass, in the usual mode, notwithstanding that transgression; but when it comes to be discussed before the *judges*, — when they consider its principles, and find it to be incompatible with the superior power of the Constitution, — it is their duty to pronounce it *void;* and judges independent, and not obliged to look to every session for a continuance of their salaries, will behave with intrepidity, and refuse to the act the sanction of judicial authority. In the same manner, the President of the United States could shield himself, and refuse to carry into effect an act that *violates* the Constitution."

It is unfortunate that the speeches of the Anti-Federalists during the latter part of the convention were suppressed; but the foregoing extracts are sufficient to show that the doctrine was clearly presented to the convention, and that it was approved by the Federalists, but neither accepted nor approved by the Anti-Federalists.

Immediately upon the close of the convention, twenty-one of the twenty-three Anti-Federalists joined in an Address and Reasons of Dissent, in which they argue: [37]

"The supremacy of the laws of the United

States is established by article sixth, viz., . . .
[quoting from the Constitution]. It has been
alleged that the words 'pursuant to the Constitution' are a restriction upon the authority
of Congress; but when it is considered that
by other sections they are invested with every
efficient power of government, and which may
be exercised to the absolute destruction of the
state governments, without any violation of
even the forms of the Constitution, this seem-
ing restriction, as well as every other restriction
in it, appears to us to be nugatory and delu-
sive; and only introduced as a blind upon the
real nature of the government. In our opinion, 'pursuant to the Constitution' will be
co-extensive with the *will* and *pleasure* of Congress, which, indeed, will be the only limitation
of their powers."

By midsummer of 1788 eleven States had
ratified the Constitution and the Union was
an established fact. The Anti-Federalists of
Pennsylvania continued their activities during the interval, but gradually changed their
method of attack, agitating not for rejection,
but for amendment. On September 3 they
assembled thirty-three delegates at Harris-
burg and adopted resolutions urging twelve

amendments, of which the first and tenth are especially significant:

"I. That congress shall not exercise any powers whatsoever, but such as are expressly given to that body by the Constitution of the United States; nor shall any authority, power or jurisdiction, be assumed or exercised by the executive or judiciary departments of the union under color or pretense of construction or fiction. But all the rights of sovereignty which are not by the said Constitution expressly and plainly vested in the congress, shall be deemed to remain with, and shall be exercised, by the several States in the union according to their respective constitutions.

"X. That congress establish no court other than the supreme court, except such as shall be necessary for determining causes of admiralty jurisdiction."

During this entire period the newspapers had been full of letters for and against the Constitution. Pamphlets were also published by individual writers. Among the first of the pamphleteers appeared Peletiah Webster, who printed "Weakness of Brutus Exposed," November, 1787, in support of the Constitution, arguing: [38]

"5. Brutus all along sounds his objections, and fears, on extreme cases of abuse or misapplication of supreme power, which may possibly happen, under the administration of a wild, weak, or wicked congress; but 't is easy to observe that all institutions are liable to extremes, but ought not to be judged by them; they do not often appear, and perhaps never may; but if they should happen in the cases supposed, (which God forbid) there is a remedy pointed out in the Constitution itself.

" 'T is not supposable that such abuses could arise to any ruinous height, before they would affect the States so much, that at least two-thirds of them would unite in pursuing a remedy in the mode prescribed by the Constitution, which will always be liable to amendment, whenever any mischiefs or abuses appear in the government, which the Constitution in its present state, can't reach and correct."

One of the ablest Anti-Federal publicists was "Centinel," whose identity has never been disclosed. His letters were printed in the *Independent Gazeteer* from October 5, 1787, to November 24, 1788. In Letter VIII, published December 29, 1787, he writes: [39]

"The authors of the present conspiracy are

attempting to seize upon absolute power at one grasp. . . . They have even exposed some of their batteries prematurely, for the unlimited power of taxation would alone have been amply sufficient for every purpose; . . . therefore there was no use in portraying the ultimate object by superadding the form to reality of supremacy in the following clause, viz.: That which empowers the new congress to make all laws that may be necessary and proper for carrying into execution any of their powers, by virtue of which every possible law will be constitutional, as they are to be the sole judges of the propriety of such laws."

> His Letter XVI, published February 23, 1788, is a curious and rather hysterical document, arguing that the constitutional prohibition against *ex post facto* laws would prevent the new government from calling public defaulters to account. He proceeds: [40]

"It may be said that the new congress would rather break through the Constitution than suffer the public to be defrauded of so much treasure, . . . but this is not to be expected. . . . Besides, should congress be disposed to violate the fundamental articles of the Constitution for the sake of public justice, . . .

still it would be of no avail, as there is a further barrier interposed between the public and these defaulters, namely, the supreme court of the union, whose province it would be to determine the constitutionality of any law that may be controverted; and supposing no bribery or corrupt influence practiced on the bench of judges, it would be their sworn duty to refuse their sanction to laws made in the face and contrary to the letter and spirit of the Constitution, as any law to compel the settlement of accounts and payment of moneys depending and due under the old confederation would be. The 1st section of the 3d article gives the supreme court cognizance of not only the laws, but of all cases arising under the Constitution, which empowers this tribunal to decide upon the construction of the Constitution itself in the last resort. This is so extraordinary, so unprecedented an authority, that the intention in vesting of it must have been to put it out of the power of congress, even by breaking through the Constitution, to compel these defaulters to restore the public treasure."

This letter is directed *against* the Constitution; so that while "Centinel" may have been

educated out of his earlier view, perhaps by a
study of Wilson's speeches, he does not appear
to regard judicial control as a desirable feature.

NEW JERSEY ratified December 18, 1787,
and GEORGIA followed January 2, 1788, both
unanimously.

CONNECTICUT fell into line a week later by
the decisive vote of 128 to 40. The question
of judicial control was briefly mentioned in
the convention. Not much has been preserved
of the Connecticut debates, but the speech by
Ellsworth above mentioned covers the issue
clearly.

The more popular view was presented in
the newspapers. The New Haven *Gazette* of
November 8, 1787, published a letter by "An
American Citizen" (dated Philadelphia, September 29, and doubtless circulated in Pennsylvania also), containing the following:

"In pursuing the consideration of the new
federal Constitution, it remains now to examine the nature and powers of the house of
representatives, the immediate delegates of the
people. . . .

"They alone can originate bills for drawing
forth the revenues of the union, and they will

have a negative upon every legislative act of the other branch. So far, in short, as the sphere of federal jurisdiction extends, they will be controulable only by the people, and in contentions with the other branch, so far as they shall be right, they must ever finally prevail."

Another Pennsylvania author, identified as Noah Webster, was quoted in the issue of November 29, 1787:

"The idea that congress can levy taxes at pleasure is false, and the suggestion wholly unsupported. The preamble to the Constitution is declaratory of the purposes of our union; and the assumption of any powers not necessary to establish justice, insure domestic tranquility, provide for the common defence, promote the general welfare, and to secure the blessings of liberty to ourselves and our posterity, will be unconstitutional and endanger the existence of congress." [41]

The issue of November 22, 1787, contains the following, by "A Countryman," identified by Mr. Paul Leicester Ford as Roger Sherman: [42]

"On examining the new proposed Constitution, there can not be a question, but that there is authority enough lodged in the proposed federal congress, if abused, to do the greatest injury. . . .

"But if the members of congress are to be interested just as you and I are, and just as the members of our present legislatures are interested, we shall be just as safe, with even supreme power (if that were granted) in congress, as in the general assembly. If the members of congress can take no improper step which will not affect them as much as it does us, we need not apprehend that they will usurp authorities not given them to injure that society of which they are a part."

MASSACHUSETTS. When the question of ratification came to an issue in Massachusetts, in January and February, 1788, the easy part of the Federalists' work was over. With the exception of Maryland, they could hope for no more one-sided victories. South Carolina was promising; but Rhode Island was hopeless, North Carolina was hostile, and New Hampshire had elected a convention with a majority instructed against ratification. Even with the adherence of Maryland and South Carolina, therefore, the ratifying States would number only seven and would include but one of the large and powerful States. The real struggle began in Massachusetts and was continued in Virginia and New York, for without the support of all three of these States a central government, if created at all, would have but a doubtful chance of success. The action of these three States is, therefore, of special interest.

The question of restraining unconstitutional action by Congress was first discussed in the Massachusetts convention by James Bowdoin, of Boston, who argued that usurpation would be prevented by the following checks: [43]

(1) Election by the people; (2) the oath taken by federal officers; (3) impeachment; (4) ineligibility for other office during their term; (5) prohibition of titles of nobility; (6) guarantee of a republican form of government; (7) division of Congress into two branches; (8) President's veto; (9) publicity of proceedings; (10) character of men to be elected; (11) the fact that Congressmen will themselves be subject to their own laws.

Theophilus Parsons, continuing the discussion, added: [44]

"The Hon. Gentleman from Boston has stated at large most of the checks the people have against usurpation, and the abuse of power [by Congress] under the proposed constitution. . . . But there is another check, founded in the nature of the union, superior to all the parchment checks that can be invented. If there should be a usurpation, it will not be upon the farmer and merchant, employed and attentive only to their several occupations, it will be upon thirteen legislatures, completely organized, possessed of the confidence of the people, and having the means, as well as inclination, successfully to oppose it. Under these circumstances, none but mad men would attempt an usurpation. But, sir, the people themselves have it in their power effectually to resist usurpation; without being driven to an appeal to arms. An act of usurpation is not obligatory, it is not law, and any man may be justified in his resistance. Let him be considered as a criminal by the general government, yet only his own fellow citizens can convict him — they are his jury, and if they pronounce him innocent, not all the powers of congress can hurt him."

Samuel Adams took little part in the debate during the first days of the session. Like most of the radicals he was an Anti-Federalist, and unless he could be persuaded to modify his opinions and vote for ratification, the Constitution had little chance of being adopted by Massachusetts. His influence was strong enough in the evenly balanced convention to be the decisive factor; and his view may be considered not only representative, but also of the first importance in guiding immediate action in the convention and future action in Congress. Toward the close of the session he indicated his intention to support the Constitution, urging at the same time amendments limiting the powers of the general government and defining those of the States. He said: [45]

"Your Excellency's first proposition is, 'that it be explicitly declared, that all powers not expressly delegated to congress are reserved to the several States, to be by them exercised.' This appears, to my mind, to be a summary of a bill of rights, which gentlemen are anxious to obtain. It removes a doubt which many have entertained respecting the matter, and gives assurance that, if any law made by the federal government shall be extended beyond the power granted by the proposed Constitution, and inconsistent with the constitution of this State, it will be an error, and adjudged by the courts of law to be void.

"It is consonant with the second article in

the present confederation, that each State retains its sovereignty, freedom and independence, and every power, jurisdiction and right, which is not by this confederation expressly delegated to the United States in congress assembled. I have long considered the watchfulness of the people over their rulers the strongest guard against the encroachments of power; and I hope the people of this country will always be thus watchful."

Although Adams does not expressly say *state* courts, the strong inference is that he referred to state courts only and was so understood by the convention. He was discussing not checks and balances in the federal machinery, but limitations to be imposed on the national government in favor of the States; and he mentions this action of "the courts of law" as a primary instance of the exercise of a reserved power by the States.

That his view was adopted by the convention, and that the plan of leaving the control of congressional legislation to the state courts was endorsed, is further indicated by the course of William Symmes, of Andover. At first Symmes was opposed to the Constitution on the ground that it gave the federal government too much power. Discussing the grant of powers to Congress, he said: [46]

"Here, Sir, (however kindly congress may be pleased to deal with us) is a very good and valid conveyance of all the property in the United States — to certain uses, indeed, but those uses capable of any construction the trustees may think proper to make. This body is not amenable to any tribunal, and therefore this congress can do no wrong."

But after the introduction of the amendments and Adams's speech, he declared: "Upon the whole, Mr. President, approving the amendments, and firmly believing that they will be adopted, I recall my former opposition." [47]

Even with the support of Adams and his followers, the vote was close, 187 to 168, but finally on February 6, 1788, the Constitution was ratified. The ratification was in the form of a resolution, declaring that we, the convention, do "ratify the said Constitution for the United States of America. And as it is the opinion of this Convention, that certain amendments and alterations in the said Constitution would . . . more effectually guard against an undue administration of the federal government, the Convention do therefore recommend . . .

"I. That it be explicitly declared that all powers not expressly delegated by the aforesaid Constitution are reserved to the several States, to be by them exercised." [48]

In MARYLAND the Federalists knew they had a majority and resolutely declined to debate. The organization of the convention occupied three days, and a day and a half were taken by the Anti-Federalists to express their opposition, so that ratification was carried on the fifth day, April 26, 1788, by a vote of 63 to 11. An attempt was then made by the minority to get a hearing for various amendments, but the proceedings ran foul of a point of order and the obvious impatience of the delegates, and the convention by a vote of 47 to 27 adjourned without acting on the amendments. [49]

Twelve members, including Luther Martin, published an account of the proceedings, with the proposed amendments, which included:

"1. That congress shall exercise no power but what is expressly delegated by this Constitution.

"6. That the federal courts shall not be

entitled to jurisdiction by fictions or collusion."

It appears from the report that both of these proposals had the approval of a considerable number of Federalists, but they became entangled in questions of procedure and were never voted on. They were, however, published in the newspapers of various other States.

In electing the delegates who pursued this course, the people of Maryland had before them Luther Martin's letter already quoted, and also a paper by Alexander Contee Hanson, afterwards a member of the convention, who under the name "Aristides" wrote as follows: [50]

"I take the construction of these words [Const., Art. I, sec. 8, § 18] to be precisely the same, as if the clause had preceded [sic] further and said, 'No act of congress shall be valid, unless it have relation to the foregoing powers, and be necessary and proper for carrying them into execution.' But say the objectors, 'The congress, being itself to judge of the necessity and propriety, may pass any act, which it may deem expedient, for any other purpose.' The objection applies with equal force to each particular power, defined by the Constitution;

and, if there were a bill of rights, congress might be said to be the judge of that also. They may reflect however, that every judge in the union, whether of federal or of state appointment, (and some persons would say every jury) will have a right to reject any act, handed to him as a law, which he may conceive to be repugnant to the Constitution."

In SOUTH CAROLINA the Constitution was read and discussed in the House of Representatives before the ratifying convention was summoned. John Julius Pringle, afterwards a member of the convention, addressing the House, said: [51]

"The treaties will affect all the individuals equally of all the States.

"If the President and senate make such as violate the fundamental laws, and subvert the Constitution, or tend to the destruction of the happiness and liberty of the States, the evils, equally oppressing all, will be removed as soon as felt, as those who are oppressed have the power and means of redress. Such treaties, not being made with good faith, and on the broad basis of reciprocal interest and convenience, but by treachery and a betraying of trust, and by exceeding the powers with which the makers were intrusted, ought to be annulled. No nations would keep treaties thus made."

Edward Rutledge, also a member of the convention, spoke on the same subject, as follows: [52]

"But the gentleman had said, that there were points in this new confederation which would endanger the rights of the people — that the President and ten senators may make treaties. . . . It was true, that the President, with the concurrence of two-thirds of the senate might make treaties, and it was possible that ten senators might constitute the two-thirds, but it was just within the reach of possibility, and a possibility from whence no danger could be apprehended; if the President or the senators abused their trust, they were answerable for their conduct — they were liable to impeachment and punishment."

Charles Pinckney, a member of the constitutional convention, discussing before the state convention the powers of the President, the Senate, and the House of Representatives (but not the judiciary) said: [53]

"With this powerful influence of the purse, they [the House] will always be able to restrain the usurpations of the other departments, while their own licentiousness will, in its turn, be checked and corrected by them."

Ratification was adopted May 23, 1788, by a vote of 149 to 73.

The following resolution was also adopted:

"This convention doth also declare that no section or paragraph of the said Constitution warrants a construction that the States do not retain every power not expressly relinquished by them, and vested in the general government of the Union." [54]

NEW HAMPSHIRE. The New Hampshire convention met early in the year with a majority opposed to ratification or instructed against it. After some discussion the members, by a majority of 3, decided to adjourn till June, in order to find out what action Massachusetts would take. During the interval the debates in the Massachusetts convention were fully reported in the New Hampshire *Gazette*. When the convention reassembled, it voted ratification 57 to 46, and adopted recommendations for amendment virtually identical with those of Massachusetts.

With the vote of New Hampshire, the existence of the United States became a legal fact; but practically the action of Virginia and

New York remained almost as important as before.

VIRGINIA. Mention has already been made of the arguments of Edmund Randolph and George Mason in the Virginia convention. John Marshall voiced the doctrine of judicial control: [55]

"Has the government of the United States power to make laws on every subject? . . . Can they go beyond the delegated powers? If they were to make a law not warranted by any of the powers enumerated, it would be considered by the judges as an infringement of the Constitution which they are to guard. They would not consider such a law as coming under their jurisdiction. They would declare it void. . . . To what quarter will you look for protection from an infringement on the Constitution, if you will not give the power to the judiciary? There is no other power that can afford such a protection."

William Grayson, on the other hand, evidently thought that judicial decision would not be final: [56]

"In England they have great courts, which have great and interfering powers. But the controlling power of parliament, which is a *central focus*, corrects them. But here each party is to shift for itself. There is no arbiter or power to correct their interference. Recurrence can be only had to the sword."

Wilson Nicholas argued that the final check would be the ballot: [57]

"The State legislatures, also, will be a powerful check on them: every new power given to congress is taken from the State legislatures; they will be, therefore, very watchful over them; for, should they exercise any power not vested in them, it will be a usurpation of the rights of the different State legislatures, who would sound the alarm to the people."

H. Lee, of Westmoreland, referred to the question in broad terms: [58]

"When a question arises with respect to the legality of any power exercised or assumed by congress, it is plain on the side of the governed: *Is it enumerated in the Constitution?* If it be, it is legal and just. It is otherwise arbitrary and unconstitutional."

Edmund Pendleton recognized judicial annulment as having occurred in the State, but did not rely on it: [59]

"My brethren in that department [the judicial] felt great uneasiness in their minds to violate the Constitution by such a law. They have prevented the operation of some unconstitutional acts. Notwithstanding those violations, I rely upon the principles of the government — that it will produce its own reform, by the responsibility resulting from frequent elections."

George Nicholas said: [60]

"Who is to determine the extent of such powers? I say, the same power which, in all well-regulated communities, determines the extent of legislative powers. If they exceed these powers, the judiciary will declare it void, or else the people will have a right to declare it void."

Patrick Henry was the leader of the Anti-Federalists and was on his feet constantly in opposition to the Constitution. He usually argued on such broad grounds that he did not touch the specific point of judicial control; but his view appears to have been that while the federal courts might on occasion declare an act of Congress unconstitutional, the chief reliance of the people ought to be based on the state judiciary. His remarks were as follows: [61]

"The honorable gentleman did our judiciary honor in saying that they had firmness to counteract the legislature in some cases. Yes, sir, our judges opposed the acts of the legislature. We have this landmark to guide us. They had the fortitude to declare that they were the judiciary, and would oppose unconstitutional acts. Are you sure that your federal judiciary will act thus? ... I take it as the highest encomium on this country, that the acts of the legislature, if unconstitutional, are liable to be opposed by the judiciary. ...

"I consider the Virginia judiciary as one of the best barriers against strides of power. ... So small are the barriers against the encroachments and usurpations of congress, that, when I see this last barrier — the independency of the judges — impaired [by appointing them federal judges at the same time, as it was suggested might be done for economy], I am persuaded I see the prostration of all our rights. ... When congress, by virtue of this sweeping clause, will organize these courts, they cannot depart from the Constitution; and their laws in opposition to the Constitution would be void. If congress, under the specious pretence of pursuing this clause, altered it, and prohibited appeals as to fact, the federal judges, if they spoke the sentiments of independent men, would declare their prohibition nugatory and void."

On June 25, 1788, the convention adopted 89 to 79, a resolution which declared that "the powers granted under the Constitution, being derived from the people of the United States, may be resumed by them whenever the same shall be perverted to their injury or oppression, and that every power not granted thereby remains with them and at their will; that, therefore, no right, of any denomination, can be cancelled, abridged, restrained, or modified, by the Congress . . . or any department or officer of the United States, except in those instances in which power is given by the Constitution for those purposes. . . . With these impressions we, the delegates, ratify the Constitution." [62] They thereupon adopted also a bill of rights containing twenty paragraphs and a series of proposed amendments which included the following: [63]

"14th. That the judicial power of the United States shall be vested in one supreme court, and in such courts of admiralty as congress may from time to time ordain and establish in any of the different States. The judicial power shall extend to all cases in law and equity arising under treaties," including cases between States, cases where the United States or an ambassador is a party, and admiralty cases.

It is noteworthy that this fourteenth amendment did not include cases arising under the laws and Constitution of the United States.

In Virginia, as in other States, a crop of pamphlets and newspaper articles sprang up, among which was Richard Harry Lee's "Letters of a Federal Farmer." In Letter IV, dated October 12, 1787, arguing against ratification, he writes: [64]

"By the article before recited [Art. VI], treaties also made under the authority of the United States, shall be the supreme law: It is not said that these treaties shall be made in pursuance of the Constitution — nor are there any constitutional bounds set to those who shall make them: The President and two-thirds of the senate will be empowered to make treaties indefinitely, and when these treaties shall be made, they will also abolish all law and State constitutions incompatible with them. This power in the President and senate is absolute, and the judges will be bound to allow full force to whatever rule, article or thing the President and senate shall establish by treaty. . . ."

The author of these letters was one of the first Senators from Virginia and a member of the judiciary committee which framed the act of 1789.

NEW YORK. The theory of judicial control was fully expounded by Alexander Hamilton in Number 78 of the *Federalist*. But in the state convention the question seems never squarely to have arisen, and even Hamilton, though arguing that an unconstitutional law would not be binding, does not indicate by whom the statute would be pronounced unconstitutional.[65] Most of the debate that approached this issue turned on the corruption of Congress or oppression through laws within the letter of the Constitution construed as it was supposed that a centralized government might interpret it.[66] It may fairly be inferred, however, from the following speech of Melancthon Smith, one of the Anti-Federalist leaders, that he considered that Congress would interpret the Constitution for itself, and that the federal as well as state courts would be bound to give effect to all federal statutes:[67]

"Whether then the general government would have a right to control the States in taxation, was a question which depended upon the construction of the Constitution. . . . No such important point should be left to doubt and construction. The clause should be so formed as to render the business of legislation as simple and plain as possible. It was not to be expected, that the members of the federal legislature would generally be versed in those subtilties, which distinguish the profession of the law. They would not be disposed to make nice distinctions, with respect to jurisdiction. . . . They would have power to abrogate the laws of the States, and to prevent the operation of their taxes; and all courts, before whom any disputes on these points should come, whether federal or not, would be bound by oath to give judgment according to the laws of the union."

By a vote of 30 to 27 the convention ratified the Constitution July 26, 1788, prefixing to the formal statement of ratification a bill of rights declared to be consistent with the Constitution, and adding a series of amendments which the New York representatives in Congress were enjoined to secure. The bill of rights contains the following: [68]

"That every power, jurisdiction, and right, which is not by the said Constitution clearly delegated to the congress of the United States, or the departments of the government thereof, remains to the people of the several States, or to their respective State governments, to whom they may have granted the same. . . .

"That the jurisdiction of the supreme court of the United States, or of any other court to be instituted by congress, is not in any case to be increased, enlarged, or extended, by any fiction, collusion, or mere suggestion."

And the amendments include: [69]

"That the congress shall not constitute, ordain or establish any tribunals or inferior courts, with any other than appellate jurisdiction, except such as may be necessary for the trial of cases of admiralty and maritime jurisdiction, and for the trial of piracies and felonies committed on the high seas; and in all other cases to which the judicial power of the United States extends, and in which the supreme court of the United States has not original jurisdiction, the causes shall be heard, tried, and determined in some of the State courts, with the right of appeal to the supreme court of the United States, or other proper tribunal, to be established for the purpose by the congress, with such exceptions, and under such regulations, as congress shall make."

The New York newspapers published letters arguing all sides of the question. In the *Journal* of January 17, 1788, we find the following by "Countryman":

"I might have saved myself a world of trouble, in searching to find out the meaning of the new Constitution, if I had only attended a little more closely at first, to that clause which says, the congress shall have power to lay and collect taxes, duties, imposts, and excises, to pay the debts and provide for the common defence and general welfare of the United States — and the other clause, which gives them power to make all laws that shall be necessary and proper for carrying into execution the foregoing powers, and all other powers, vested by this constitution in the government of the United States, or in any department or officer thereof. The first gives them power to do any thing at all, if they only please to say, it is for the common welfare, for they are the only judges of this."

The argument in favor of vesting judicial control in the courts was fully and cogently presented by Alexander Hamilton in the *Fed-*

eralist series, while the opposite view was strongly urged by Robert Yates [70] writing as "Brutus." A brief extract from Yates has already been quoted. The *Federalist* papers are too well known and too readily accessible to justify a more extended reference; but as the Brutus letters have never to my knowledge been reprinted, and as they prophesy with remarkable accuracy the development of judicial power that would result from vesting in the courts the authority to decide upon the constitutionality of statutes, I add several paragraphs from Letters XI and XV. In the light of current discussion, they might well be reprinted in full.

"XI. This government is a complete system, not only for making, but for executing laws. And the courts of law, which will be constituted by it, are not only to decide upon the Constitution and the laws made in pursuance of it, but by officers subordinate to them, to execute all their decisions. The real effect of this system of government will therefore be brought home to the feelings of the people through the medium of the judicial power. . . . No errors they may commit can be corrected by any power above them, if any such power there be, nor can they be removed from office for making ever so many erroneous decisions. . . .

"From these remarks [discussion of Art. 3, § 2], the authority and business of the courts of law, under this clause may be understood.

"They will give the sense of every article of the Constitution that may from time to time come before them. And in their decisions they will not confine themselves to any fixed or established rules, but will determine according to what appears to them the reason and spirit of the Constitution. The opinions of the supreme court, whatever they may be, will have the force of law; because there is no power provided in the Constitution, that can correct their errors or control their jurisdiction. From this court there is no appeal. And I conceive the legislature themselves cannot set aside a judgment of this court, because they are authorized by the Constitution to decide in the last resort. . . .

" The judicial power will operate to effect in the most certain but silent and imperceptible manner what is evidently the tendency of the Constitution — I mean, an entire subversion of the legislative, executive and judicial powers of the individual States. Every adjudication of the supreme court, on any question that may arise upon the nature and extent of the general government, will affect the limits of the State jurisdiction. In proportion as the former enlarge the exercise of their powers, will that of the latter be restricted.

"That the judicial power of the United States will lean strongly in favor of the general government, and will give such an explanation to the Constitution, as will favor an extension of its jurisdiction, is very evident from a variety of considerations."

"XV. The power of this court is in many cases superior to that of the legislature. I have shewed in a former paper that this court will be authorized to decide upon the meaning of the Constitution, and that not only according to the natural and ob[sic — obvious?] meaning of the words, but also according to the spirit and intention of it. In the exercise of this power they will be not subordinate to but above the legislature. . . . The supreme court then have a right, independent of the legislature, to give a construction to the Constitution and every part of it, and there is no power provided in this system to correct their construction or do away with it. If therefore the legislature pass any laws inconsistent with the sense the judges put upon the Constitution, they will declare it void; and therefore in this respect their power is superior to that of the legislature."

Although NORTH CAROLINA did not ratify until November 21, 1789, after the close of the first session of Congress, yet her attitude had its effect upon the political situation. Madison and other leading statesmen were anxious to bring both North Carolina and Rhode Island into the Union as quickly as possible, and kept constantly in mind the effect of both Congressional legislation and constitutional amendment upon those States. In the first North Carolina convention several Federalists discussed Congressional usurpation. John Steele said: [71]

"The judicial power of that government is so well constructed as to be a check. There was no check in the old confederation. Their power was, in principle and theory, transcendent. If the congress make laws inconsistent with the Constitution, independent judges will not uphold them, nor will the people obey them. A universal resistance will ensue."

Archibald Maclaine did not accept judicial control: [72]

"We know now that it is agreed upon by most writers, and men of judgment and reflection, that all power is in the people, and immediately derived from them. . . . If congress should make a law beyond the powers and the spirit of the Constitution, should we not say to congress, 'You have no authority to make this law. There are limits beyond which you cannot go. You cannot exceed the power prescribed by the Constitution. You are amenable to us for your conduct. This act is unconstitutional. We will disregard it, and punish you for the attempt.'"

James Iredell, quoted by all writers as one of the stanchest champions of judicial control, did not urge it in the convention; he argued that *the people* would restrain Congressional usurpation: [73]

"Every individual in the United States will keep his eye watchfully over those who administer the general government, and no usurpation of power will be acquiesced in. The possibility of usurping powers ought not to be objected against it [the Constitution]. Abuse may happen in any government. The only resource against usurpation is the inherent right of the people to prevent its exercise. This is the case in all free governments in the world. The people will resist if the government usurp powers not delegated to it."

This first convention adjourned August 1, 1788, after rejecting the Constitution by a vote of 184 to 84. The ground of disapproval was indicated by a resolution demanding a bill of rights and "amendments to the most ambiguous and exceptionable parts of the said Constitution." The proposed amendments include the following: [74]

"1. That each State in the Union shall respectively retain every power, jurisdiction and right, which is not by this Constitution delegated to the congress of the United States or to the departments of the federal government.

"15. That the judicial power of the United States shall be vested in one supreme court, and in such courts of admiralty as congress may from time to time ordain and establish in any of the different States," etc., limiting the jurisdiction to cases arising under treaties and between certain parties. (This amendment is identical with Virginia's fourteenth.)

RHODE ISLAND took no action whatever until

May 29, 1790, when she ratified and at the same time proposed amendments similar to North Carolina's bill of rights and first amendment; but as neither the debate in the convention nor its action could have influenced Congress directly, I will not extend this paper by any quotations. But during the period of inaction by the Rhode Island authorities, the people were discussing the Constitution; and the following qualified approval of judicial control was published by "Solon Junior" in the *Providence Gazette and Country Journal* of August 9, 1788:

"An abundance of proof lies within our own observation, of the prevalence of the spirit of the times over the dead letter of laws and constitutions. During the war, and while that was the rage of the day, was not an act passed for putting every free-man in the State under martial law, to be inflicted by a general over whom even the legislature had no control? — yet the people bore it — and those who complained of its being unconstitutional were answered, that the safety of the people is the highest law. . . ."

The writer proceeded to discuss the case of *Trevett* v. *Weeden*, in which the state court had

held unconstitutional a law limiting trial by
jury, and the action of the voters in ousting
the judges. "Had that privilege [trial by jury],"
he continued, "been ever so safe on paper,
and a phrenzy seized the administration similar
to that under which this State at a certain time
laboured, could not a penal law have passed
congress, and been enforced by a federal court
— or a federal army — unless, indeed, they
should have found the unconquerable spirit of
an Adams in that court, to humble the pride of
usurped power?"

To sum up this partial survey of the evi-
dences of popular intent, from the adjourn-
ment of the constitutional convention to the
opening of the First Congress, I conclude:
(1) That the theory of judicial control was
sufficiently familiar to be presented to the conventions of most of the States; (2) that the
Federalists on the whole accepted, but did not
strongly urge it; (3) that the Anti-Federalists
either did not accept it or else found in it an
argument against ratification; (4) that in no
convention was it a conspicuous issue, that in
several it was not considered seriously, if at
all, and that in none was it a question which
presumably influenced votes or on which the

State took a specific stand; (5) that to all intents and purposes it was swallowed up in the larger question of state rights; (6) that the States which proposed amendments in the spirit of the Tenth Amendment (Massachusetts, South Carolina, New Hampshire, Virginia, New York and North Carolina — besides substantial minorities in Pennsylvania and Maryland) intended thereby to make the States rather than the federal judiciary the guardians of the Constitution; (7) that the jealousy of federal authority on the part of all of these States extended to the judiciary, and was so pronounced as to preclude the idea that the people could have contemplated vesting in the Supreme Court (much less in any inferior courts) the power to annul an act of Congress; their intent plainly was to limit the influence and activities of federal courts rather than to extend them by any possible implication. I conclude further that Congress by proposing the first ten amendments, which include — "X. The powers not delegated to the United States by the Constitution, nor prohibited by it to the States, are reserved to the States, respectively, or to the people" — and the several States by ratifying them, intended to reserve to the States the authority to decide upon the constitutionality of acts of Congress (a power which was left open by the Constitution itself, and therefore not delegated to the United States), and that the logical result of their action was to do so.

This view I consider is borne out by the terms of the judiciary act of 1789. With the realization that I am treading on dangerous ground in drawing the above conclusions and in advocating an interpretation of the judiciary act pronounced "absurd" by an able scholar, I nevertheless pass on to the consideration of that statute.

The Judiciary Act of 1789

A full discussion of the judiciary act would partake too much of the nature of a legal brief to be permissible in this article; but in any case I am concerned not with what the judges or law-writers have said about it, but with what members of the First Congress said about it and with what its language presumably meant to them. Unfortunately the annals of Congress give no record of Congressional views; nor does Maclay's *Journal*, nor any newspapers I have seen. Therefore we are reduced, once for all, to the statute itself, without even any record of amendments to guide us.

A critical study of the Constitution and the statute leads me to the following conclusions: The Constitution leaves to Congress not only the organization of the entire judiciary department, but also the practical definition of its jurisdiction except in a negligible number of cases; the statute does not use apt words to give any federal court the power of annulling statutes as unconstitutional; but on the contrary, it does expressly, by an elementary canon of construction, deprive the Supreme Court of such power.

Looking first at the Constitution itself, we are reminded that the entire subject of the judiciary is left to Congress, with the single exception that there shall be a Supreme Court with original jurisdiction in all cases affecting ambassadors, public ministers and consuls, and those in which a State shall be a party; and that the "judicial power shall extend to all cases, in law and equity, arising under this Constitution, the laws of the United States, and treaties made, or which shall be made, under their authority." In other words, if Congress had decided to organize a judiciary with no inferior court except a court of admiralty, as was demanded by some of the States, and had further excepted from the appellate jurisdiction of the Supreme Court, as it had the right to do,[75] all questions of unconstitutionality, the Supreme Court could not possibly have acquired original jurisdiction over enough cases to make it an arbiter of constitutionality. It was a thousand-to-one shot that no such case would *ever* arise within the extremely narrow bounds of original jurisdiction; and perhaps that was why Chief Justice Marshall, when by extraordinary chance Marbury's case came before the Supreme Court on motion and not by appeal, went out of his way to deliver his manifesto on the annulment of unconstitutional laws. Even to-day cases of original jurisdiction are very rare; and it may well happen that the constitutionality of an act of Congress will never again be considered in such a case.

Practically, then, Congress had the situation in its own hands. Unless it wished to, there was no necessity for it to give *any* federal court authority to decide the constitutionality of *any* federal statute. It therefore seems unnecessary to discuss at all the arguments of Mr. Brinton

Coxe and his followers[76] who contend that the Constitution expressly gives the power of annulment to the Supreme Court.

Practically, then, what did Congress do? It was in a position to make the Supreme Court custodian of the Constitution or to give that authority to the States. Which did it do? The answer is contained in the judiciary act of September 24, 1789 (1 Stat. 73, chap. 20), un-illuminated by any of the usual aids to statu-tory construction — precedent, report, debate, criticism, or record of amendment.

That act is largely devoted to the mere machinery of organization — division of the country into districts, provision for sessions and officers of court, process, and like matters. Its significant features are as follows: (1) It creates the District Courts (sec. 3) with juris-diction (sec. 9) of certain crimes, admiralty and revenue, certain cases where an alien sues, certain suits brought by the United States, and suits against consuls and vice-consuls; (2) it creates the Circuit Courts (sec. 4) with jurisdiction (sec. 11) in certain suits brought by the United States, or where an alien is a party, or between citizens of different States, over certain crimes and over appeals from the

District Courts; (3) it organizes a Supreme
Court (sec. 1) with original jurisdiction (sec. 13)
cases where a State, an ambassador, public
minister, consul or vice-consul is a party, and
appellate jurisdiction from the Circuit Court
(sec. 22), and also (sec. 25) from a state court
"where is drawn in question the validity of a
treaty or statute of, or an authority exercised
under the United States, and the decision is
against their validity," and where a state
statute is questioned, and "where is drawn in
question the construction of any clause of the
Constitution, or of a treaty, or statute of, or
commission held under the United States, and
the decision is against the title, right, privilege
or exemption specially set up or claimed by
either party under such clause of the said Constitution, treaty, statute or commission."

I am unable to find in this statute, either
expressly or by implication, any grant of power
to annul an act of Congress. It is highly significant that the jurisdiction of none of the courts
is extended to "cases in law and equity arising
under this Constitution, the laws of the United
States, and treaties made, or which shall be
made, under their authority." If Congress had
intended to give the power of judicial control,

the inevitable inference is that at least the words of the Constitution would have been inserted in the statute (as they were by Randolph in his draft); intending not to give it, Congress need only omit these words. It may be argued that the insertion of these words was unnecessary; that if any courts were created, they acquired such jurisdiction by operation of the Constitution itself. This invites a highly technical line of discussion which cannot be pursued in this article; but I may express the opinion that the Constitution does not directly vest jurisdiction in any inferior court, but only describes the limits of possible jurisdiction. In any case it cannot be supposed that Congress would have left so important a matter to mere construction; and it is the intent of Congress that we are seeking — its actual, human, common sense intent, and not a fictitious intent by legal implication.

If the inferior courts had no such authority, the Supreme Court could not acquire it as a normal appellate function. Nor is such authority expressly given by the statute. On the contrary, it is expressly withheld.

The Supreme Court is given the power to reverse or affirm the decision of a state court adjudging a federal statute unconstitutional. In other words, the Supreme Court may acquiesce in the action of a State annulling a federal statute; or it may reverse the State's decision, and pronounce the law constitutional and valid. But it has no jurisdiction to decide of its own accord that the law is unconstitutional. That this result was intentional is the conclusion from one of the elementary canons of construction — that the express mention of one thing is the exclusion of another.[77] The authority to declare an act of Congress unconstitutional is expressly granted to the Supreme Court on an appeal from a state judgment so deciding; therefore it is withheld in all other cases.

To pursue this branch of the subject farther would be to invite the reader into an argument already unpardonably technical. It remains, then, only to sum up the result of my investigations.

It must be conceded, I think, that the earlier writers on this topic were too hasty in their conclusions. The evidence is convincing that judicial control was a familiar conception to many of the lawyers of 1787–89, and appealed to a majority of those who discussed it as the logical result of a written constitution. By a fair proportion it was advocated as desirable.

But the precise question of control by the United States Supreme Court over acts of Congress had a very different standing in the debate. It was opposed by all those who disapproved the aggrandizement of one branch of the government at the expense of a theoretically coördinate branch; and it was disapproved also by those who favored the retention by the States of as much power as was consistent with a stable and efficient central government.

It may also be questioned whether the theory of judicial control was widely understood or approved outside of the legal profession. It seems that most of the laymen, as well as many lawyers, regarded the question of constitutionality as political rather than legal.

The entire subject, though discussed in the constitutional convention, was left open in the Constitution. It was subordinated in those ratifying conventions of whose debates we have records, and in the newspapers of 1787–88, to the great question of state sovereignty; and the doctrine of judicial control by the Supreme Court was expressly and strongly opposed by many of the Anti-Federalists. The Constitution was ratified by so narrow a margin that it would have been a distinct breach of faith not to have adopted the Tenth Amendment, reserving to the States and the people the powers not delegated to the federal government, one of which powers was that of deciding upon the constitutionality of acts of Congress. And the spirit of that reservation was further recognized and given effect in the judiciary act, vesting in the state courts, but not in the federal courts, the power to annul acts in contravention of the Constitution.

If this reasoning is correct, we arrive by a different path at the conclusion broached by the earlier writers — that our forefathers did not give the United States Supreme Court the power to annul acts of Congress.

THE END

NOTES

NOTES

CHAPTER I

1. *Dartmouth College* v. *Woodward,* 4 Wheat. 518.
2. *Ives* v. *South Buffalo Ry.,* 201 N. Y. 271.
3. See chapter III.
4. A few days after deciding the well-known *Ives case,* 201 N. Y. 271, nullifying the workingmen's compensation act, the Court of Appeals said (*Korn* v. *Lipman,* 201 N. Y. 404) that although a man's property might be taken after mailing a proper notice in the post office, yet mailing the same notice in a letter-chute or post-box would not be due process of law.
5. *People ex rel. Crossey* v. *Grout,* 179 N. Y. 417.
6. *People ex rel. Moskowitz* v. *Jenkins,* 202 N. Y. 53.
7. *Matthews* v. *People,* 202 Ill. 389.
8. *Holden* v. *Hardy,* 169 U. S. 366.
9. *In re Kemmeler,* 136 U. S. 436.
10. *Slaughter-House cases,* 17 Wall. 36.
11. *Davidson* v. *New Orleans,* 96 U. S. 97.
12. *Hopper* v. *Stack,* 69 N. J. L. 562.
13. *State* v. *Muller,* 48 Ore. 252.
14. *Ritchie* v. *People,* 155 Ill. 98.
15. *Allgeyer* v. *Louisiana,* 165 U. S. 578, 589.
16. *Dartmouth College* v. *Woodward,* 4 Wheat. 518.
17. It took nine years to validate the eight-hour law in New York.

CHAPTER II

1. C. G. Haines, *The American Doctrine of Judicial Supremacy,* pp. 122–38. Professor Haines also reviews the early judicial decisions on constitutional law and the early political discussions. In the latter

be follows Professor Beard's *The Supreme Court and the Constitution* without much analysis.

2. See, for instance, *Kampner* v. *Hawkins*, 4 Call, 150 (Virginia, 1793); *Ogden* v. *Witherspoon*, 2 Haywood, 227 (North Carolina, 1802); *Hayburn's case*, 2 Dallas, 209 (Federal Circuit Court, 1792); and the celebrated case of *Marbury* v. *Madison*, 1 Cranch, 137 (United States Supreme Court) — in all of which the statutes in question were at least arguably valid; and *Commonwealth* v. *Caton*, 4 Call, 5 (Virginia, 1782); and *Trevett* v. *Weeden*, Varnum (Rhode Island, 1786) — where the opinions were admittedly *obiter*.

3. G. E. Walling, *Recollections of a New York Chief of Police*, pp. 56–60. For the legal aftermath, see *People ex rel. McCune* v. *Board of Police of the Metropolitan Police District*, 19 N. Y. 188.

4. Cooley, *Constitutional Limitations* (7th ed.), p. 259. Iowa and North Carolina protect their officials and Texas indicates a still broader doctrine.

5. *Sumner* v. *Beeler*, 50 Ind. 341.

6. *People* v. *Tiphaine*, 13 How. Pr. 74.

7. *Chenango Bridge Co.* v. *Paige*, 83 N. Y. 178.

8. *Ives* v. *South Buffalo Ry.*, 201 N. Y. 271.

9. *Matter of Jacobs*, 98 N. Y. 98.

10. *People* v. *Williams*, 189 N. Y. 131.

11. See Haines, chap. 14.

12. See chapter i.

13. A list of statutes with a description of my method of classifying them will be found in the Appendix.

CHAPTER III

1. It should be observed that most of the adverse criticism of courts for annulling legislation has been directed at state courts reviewing state laws. The question raised by that situation, though different from the historical question here discussed, is similar

in its present political aspects. It is probable that the state courts were greatly influenced by the opinion in *Marbury* v. *Madison*.

2. W. Clark, address, *Congressional Record*, July 31, 1911; W. Tricket, "Judicial Dispensation from Congressional Statutes," *American Law Review*, XII, 65; L. B. Boudin, "Government by Judiciary," *Political Science Quarterly*, XXVI, 238; G. Roe, "Our Judicial Oligarchy," *La Follette's Weekly Magazine*, III, no. 25, p. 7.

3. C. A. Beard, *The Supreme Court and the Constitution;* A. C. McLaughlin, *The Courts, The Constitution and Parties*.

4. Compare the reversal of attitude of many of the States at the time of the Hartford Convention of 1814.

5. 1 Cranch, 137.

6. "The president and the federal independent judges, so much concerned in the execution of the laws and in the determination of their constitutionality." Ford's *Pamphlets*, 184.

7. Ford's *Pamphlets*, 183.

8. Ford's *Pamphlets*, 212.

9. "If the general legislature should at any time overlap their limits, the judicial department is a constitutional check. If the United States go beyond their powers, if they make a law which the constitution does not authorize, it is void; and the judicial power, the national judges, who, to secure their impartiality, are to be made independent, will declare it to be void." Elliot's *Debates*, II, 196.

10. Elliot's *Debates*, I, 493.

11. Ford's *Pamphlets*, 8.

12. "The judges who are bound by oath to support the Constitution, declare against this law." Elliot's *Debates*, IV, 393.

13. *Writings*, V, 293.

14. Farrand's *Reports*, III, 172, 220.

15. *Ibid.*, III, 287.

16. Elliot's *Debates*, III, p. 479.

17. Ford's *Pamphlets*, 331.

18. K. M. Rowland, *Life of George Mason*, II, chap. 8.

19. Wharton's *State Trials*, 412.

20. Ford's *Pamphlets*, 274.

21. Elliot's *Debates*, III, 121.

22. American State Papers, Misc. I, 23.

23. 2 Dallas, 409.

24. Blair, 1782: "The court had power to declare any resolution or act of the legislature or of either branch of it, to be unconstitutional and void."

   Hamilton, 1788: "The courts of justice whose duty it must be to declare all acts contrary to the manifest tenor of the Constitution void."

   King, 1787: "The judicial ought not to join in the negative of a law because the judges will have the expounding of those laws when they come before them; and they will no doubt stop the operation of such as shall appear repugnant to the Constitution."

   G. Morris, 1787: "He could not agree that the judiciary, which was a part of the executive, should be bound to say that a direct violation of the Constitution was law."

   Williamson, 1787: "Such a prohibitory clause is in the constitution of North Carolina, and, though it has been violated, it has done good there and may do good here, because the judges can take hold of it."

   Wilson, 1788: "If a law should be made inconsistent with those powers vested by this instrument in Congress, the judges . . . will declare such law to be null and void."

25. A quotation from Sherman's "Countryman" letters, printed on pp. 83, 84, indicates that he did not rely on judicial control.

26. *New York Journal and Weekly Register*, XLII, no. 24, March 20, 1788.

27. Vol. IV, 468.

28. "It is their [the judiciary's] province to decide upon our laws, and if they find this clause to be unconstitutional, they will not hesitate to declare it so."

29. Bedford, 1787: "The representatives of the people . . . ought to be under no external control whatever."

Mercer, 1787: "He disapproved of the doctrine that the judges as expositors of the Constitution should have authority to declare a law void."

Spaight, 1787: "It is immaterial what law they [the judges] have declared void; it is their usurpation of the authority to do it that I complain of."

30. Elliot's *Debates*, I, 506.

31. J. B. Thayer's *John Marshall*, 65.

32. Elliot's *Debates*, I, 126.

33. Von Holst, *Constitutional History*, I, 63.

34. McMaster and Stone, *Pennsylvania and the Federal Constitution*, 766.

35. *Ibid.*, 255, 259, 269.

36. *Ibid.*, 445, 478, 489.

37. *Ibid.*, 562.

38. Ford's *Documents*, 126.

39. McMaster and Stone, 623.

40. *Ibid.*, 659.

41. The original is reproduced in Ford's *Pamphlets*, 25. Webster adds a footnote: "Any powers not promotive of these purposes will be unconstitutional; — consequently any appropriations of money to any other purpose will expose the congress to the resentment of the States, and the members to impeachment and the loss of their seats."

42. P. L. Ford's *Essays on the Constitution*, 211.

43. Elliot's *Debates*, II, 85.

44. *Ibid.*, 93.

45. Elliot's *Debates*, II, 131.
46. *Ibid.*, 71.
47. *Ibid.*, 174.
48. *Ibid.*, I, 322.
49. *Ibid.*, II, 549.
50. Ford's *Pamphlets*, 234.
51. Elliot's *Debates*, IV, 269.
52. *Debates on Adopting the Federal Constitution in the State of South Carolina*, 21.
53. *Ibid.*, 71.
54. Elliot's *Debates*, I, 325.
55. *Ibid.*, V, 553.
56. *Ibid.*, 563.
57. *Ibid.*, 18.
58. *Ibid.*, 186.
59. *Ibid.*, 299.
60. *Ibid.*, 443.
61. *Ibid.*, III, 325, 539, 541.
62. *Ibid.*, I, 327.
63. *Ibid.*, III, 659.
64. Ford's *Pamphlets*, 312.
65. F. Childs, *Debates and Proceedings of the Convention of the State of New York*, 113.
66. See *Speeches of John Lansing, Jr., and John Williams, ibid.*, 75, 91, 96.
67. *Ibid.*, 123.
68. Elliot's *Debates*, I, 327.
69. *Ibid.*, 331.
70. Ford's *Essays*, 295.
71. Elliot's *Debates*, IV, 71.
72. *Ibid.*, 161.
73. *Ibid.*, 185.
74. *Ibid.*, II, 244.
75. "In all the other cases before mentioned [cases within the judicial power, but where the supreme court has no original jurisdiction], the supreme court shall have appellate jurisdiction, both as to law and fact,

with such exceptions, and under such regulations, *as the congress may make.*" Constitution, Art. III, Sec. 2.

76. B. Coxe, *Judicial Power and Unconstitutional Legislation;* J. H. Dougherty, *Power of Federal Judiciary over Legislation.*

77. Stimson's *Law Dictionary — expressio unius est exclusio alterius.*

APPENDIX

APPENDIX

NEW YORK STATUTES ADJUDICATED

THE classification of statutes here attempted is based on judicial decisions to June 1, 1912.

In determining the group to which each statute should be assigned, about equal weight has been given to the subject-matter of the statute and the ground of attack. Neither of these tests is in itself wholly satisfactory.

It is almost a matter of course to argue that every statute violates the Fourteenth Amendment. If it were not for the undue weight that this line of attack would give to the "Social and Economic" group, it would be more satisfactory to base the classification wholly on the constitutional principle involved. And that method would also permit a grouping which would distinguish the laws annulled upon purely technical grounds, such as insufficient title. But after several experiments, it seemed best to adopt a few rather comprehensive headings adapted to the subject-matter of the legislation and to give weight to both the general purpose of the statute in question and the particular topic of the paragraph attacked.

Where there has been any option among the groups, the statute has always been assigned to the most specific. In order of preference, "Local and Private" have been regarded as most general;

"Administrative" and "Social and Economic" next; then "Highways and Waterways" and "Judiciary, Legislature and Military," and finally "Elections," "Public Service," and "Taxes and Assessments" as most specific.

The date of the statute does not indicate (except as a limit) when its constitutionality was passed upon; and consequently a comparison by dates cannot confidently be relied upon to prove any tendency on the part of the courts. Attention may, however, be called to the great increase of late years in the "Social and Economic" group, and the proportionately much greater increase in the number of statutes of that class adjudged unconstitutional.

A group of statutes, or a statute with a series of amendments, all relating to a single subject and all attacked together upon the same ground, is counted as one statute. The laws so grouped together are indicated by corresponding exponents, e.g. — Laws of 1906, c. 909, § 57[3]; 1909, c. 22, §122[3]; 1911, c. 891[3] — these three counting as one.

Where different parts of a single statute are attacked upon different grounds, whether in the same case or in different cases, each section adjudicated is counted as a separate statute. This is particularly true of city charters and the Consolidated Laws, all of which are for convenience tabulated like ordinary session laws.

It often happens that a single statute is pronounced unconstitutional in part only. In such cases the statute is counted for both negative and affirmative and is printed in italics in the tables.

ADMINISTRATIVE

Constitutional

Revised Laws, vol. 2, p. 368, sec. 81; p. 436, sec. 236.
Code of Civil Procedure, *sec. 709; sec. 1421.*
Laws of 1797, c. 51.

1806, c. 53.

1813, c. 86; 1816, c. 1.

1828, c. 447.

1830, c. 58^2; c. 320; 1838, c. 332.

1844, c. 315^2; 1847, c. 432; c. 426; 1849, c. 194.

1853, c. 80; *c. 230, title 8;* c. 352; c. 467; 1855, c. 407; 1857, c. 337; c. 339; c. 344; c. 405; c. 485; c. 521; c. 523; *c. 569;* 1858, c. 36; 1859, c. 302^2; c. 384.

1860, c. 509; 1861, c. 308; c. 333^2; 1863, c. 18^2; c. 227^3; c. 393; 1864, c. 402^2; 1865, c. 29; c. 249; c. 554^2; c. 564; c. 565; 1866, c. 74; c. 347^2; c. 483^2; c. 730; 1867, c. 586^3; c. 708^3; c. 956; 1868, c. 571; c. 853^3; 1869, c. 483; c. 902^3.

1870, c. 137; c. 273; c. 291; *c. 374;* c. 383, sec. 27; 1871, c. 5; c. 460; c. 485; c. 810; 1872, c. 9; c. 219; c. 293^3; c. 580; c. 771; 1873, c. 285; c. 335, sec. 2; c. 335, sec. 25; c. 335, sec. 73; c. 335, sec. 114; c. 779; 1874, c. 323; c. 547; c. 628; c. 638; 1875, c. 49; c. 300; c. 400; c. 605^2; 1877, c. 64^2; c. 459^2; 1878, c. 75; c. 317; *1879, c. 85^2;* c. 89^2; c. 213^2; c. 467^2.

1880, c. 14, sec. 179; c. 14, sec. 276; c. 284; c. 377; c. 521; 1881, c. 144^2; c. 183; c. 559; 1882, c. 344; c. 359; 1883, c. 319^2; c. 336; *c. 354^2;* c. 412; c. 465; c. 490; 1884, c. 410^2; c. 516; c. 522; 1885, c. 17; c. 270^2; c. 428; 1886, c. 120, sec. 207; c. 335; 1887, c. 462; 1888, c. 29; c. 309^2; 1889, c. 161; c. 291^2; c. 382.

1890, c. 55; c. 314^2; c. 523; 1891, c. 4^5; c. 33; c. 245; 1892, c. 54; c. 182, sec. 181; c. 358;

c. 379; c. 397; c. 466; c. 488, sec. 238; c. 556[5];
c. 603; c. 686, secs. 31–33; c. 686, sec. 37[2]; 1893,
c. 573; 1894, c. 528[5]; c. 752[5]; 1895, c. 247; c. 519[5];
c. 934; c. 975; c. 1018; 1896, c. 74; c. 178; c. 727;
c. 772; c. 902[2]; 1897, c. 108; c. 220; c. 378
(Greater New York Charter, revised by Laws of
1901, c. 466), sec. 382; sec. 475; sec. 739; sec. 998;
sec. 1172; sec. 1570; 1898, c. 182, sec. 180; c. 182,
sec. 184; c. 588; 1899, c. 128, sec. 254; c. 133[2];
c. 370; c. 624.

1900, c. 658; 1901, c. 33; c. 89; *c. 466;* c. 704[3];
c. 705[3]; c. 706[3]; 1902, c. 270; c. 506; 1905, c. 501;
c. 646; 1907, c. 429; c. 711; 1909, c. 64, sec. 53.

Unconstitutional

Code Civ. Proc., *sec. 709; sec. 1421.*
Laws of 1808, c. 216.

    1843, c. 88.

    1850, c. 262; *1853, c. 230, tit. 8;* 1854, c. 386;
1857, c. 569, sec. 20; 1858, c. 321.

    1860, c. 449; 1866, c. 214, tit. 2, sec. 2; c. 217;
c. 586; 1867, c. 410; c. 806; 1868, c. 45; c. 553[2];
1869, c. 96[2].

    1870, c. 77; *c. 374;* c. 467; c. 700; 1871, c. 385;
c. 566; 1873, c. 638; 1878, c. 253; *1879, c. 85.*

    1881, c. 456; 1882, c. 251; 1883, c. 354.

    1893, c. 148; 1895, c. 344; *c. 934; c. 1018;* 1896,
c. 424; c. 427; *c. 772;* 1898, c. 398; *1899, c. 370,
sec. 13;* c. 687.

    1901, c. 178; *c. 466;* 1902, c. 127; c. 473; 1903,
c. 383; c. 515; 1904, c. 629; 1906, c. 431; 1912,
c. 548.

ELECTIONS

Constitutional

Laws of 1853, c. 80; 1858, c. 22.

    1865, c. 365, tit. 9, sec. 18; 1869, c. 912, tit. 3,
sec. 10.

1872, c. 575; 1873, c. 84.
1891, c. 105, sec. 271[2]; 1895, c. 805[2].
1905, c. 689; 1908, c. 521; 1909, c. 22, sec. 123; *1911, c. 649.*

Unconstitutional

Laws of 1867, c. 194.
1892, c. 214.
1906, c. 909, sec. 57[3]; 1907, c. 538; 1909, c. 22, sec. 122[3]; sec. 136; sec. 159; sec. 194[2]; sec. 331; *1911, c. 649[2]; c. 891[3].*

HIGHWAYS AND WATERWAYS

Constitutional

Rev. Laws, vol. 2, p. 412; 440, sec. 178; Rev. Stat., vol. 1, p. 226, sec. 49; 512, secs. 68–74.
Laws of 1817, c. 262; 1819, c. 18.
1823, c. 111; 1826, c. 185, sec. 54.
1830, c. 56; c. 135; 1833, c. 319[2]; 1838, c. 156[2].
1845, c. 181[2]; 1846, c. 244; 1847, c. 455[2]; 1848, c. 90; 1849, c. 352[2].
1850, c. 158; c. 283; 1853, c. 62; 1854, c. 87; 1855, c. 164; *c. 296;* 1857, c. 136; c. 267[2]; c. 417; c. 498; c. 639.
1860, c. 488[2]; 1861, c. 340[2]; 1862, c. 487; 1864, c. 25; c. 547; 1866, c. 367; 1867, c. 697; c. 945; 1869, c. 262[2]; c. 855[3].
1870, c. 55; c. 160; c. 291, tit. 7, sec. 2[2]; c. 373; c. 623[3]; 1871, c. 340[2]; c. 674[3]; 1872, c. 285[3]; c. 500[3]; c. 872; 1873, c. 323[3]; c. 528; 1874, c. 256; c. 287; c. 604; c. 647; 1875, c. 2; c. 91; c. 482; c. 604[2]; 1876, c. 135[2]; c. 147[2]; c. 445; 1877, c. 165; 1878, c. 171; c. 190; c. 410[3]; 1879, c. 253[2]; c. 345[2].
1880, c. 318[3]; 1881, c. 326[3]; c. 469; c. 554; 1882, c. 410, sec. 86; c. 410, secs. 715–716; 1884, c. 187[2]; c. 534[3]; c. 546[2]; 1885, c. 414[2]; c. 451; c.

499³; 1886, c. 658; 1887, c. 113; c. 136; c. 205; c. 557; c. 716³; 1888, c. 193; c. 325.

1890, c. 249; c. 315; c. 568, sec. 89; *1892, c. 411;* c. 493; 1893, c. 537; c. 694²; 1895, c. 1006; 1896, c. 338.

1903, c. 147; 1904, c. 734; 1905, c. 476; 1910, c. 701.

Unconstitutional

Rev. Laws, vol. 2, p. 238²; 416, sec. 179; Rev. Stat., vol. I, p. 513, sec. 77; 3, p. 318².

Laws of 1801, c. 127².

1813, c. 62².

1847, c. 375; 1849, c. 184, secs. 60–64.

1850, c. 264; 1851, c. 207²; c. 485; 1855, c. 164; *c. 296.*

1868 c. 522; c. 687; c. 717; c. 776; 1869, c. 507; c. 670; c. 850; c. 880.

1870, c. 291, tit. 7³; c. 543; c. 593; 1878, c. 59³.

1880, c. 114; 1881, c. 303²; 1882, c. 410, sec. 677.

1890, c. 568, secs. 106–116; 1891, c. 136²; c. 290; *1892, c. 411;* 1893, c. 694³; 1894, c. 712²; 1897, c. 286.

1901, c. 466; 1906, c. 419; 1907, c. 93.

JUDICIARY, LEGISLATURE, AND MILITARY

Constitutional

Revised Laws, vol. 2, p. 408, sec. 177; 507, sec. 8.

Rev. Stat., vol. 1, p. 154, secs. 13–14; 638, sec. 9²; vol. 2, p. 516, sec. 47; 727, sec. 50.

Code of Procedure, sec. 6; *sec. 30;* sec. 33; sec. 62; sec. 167; sec. 282; sec. 288.

Code Civ. Proc., sec. 134; sec. 162; sec. 234; sec. 432; sec. 435; *sec. 791²; sec. 793²;* secs. 856–857; sec. 873²; sec. 970²; secs. 1422–1425; sec. 1778; sec. 2122; sec. 2706; secs. 2798–2799.

Code Crim. Proc., sec. 8; sec. 56; sec. 281; secs. 293–295; sec. 313; sec. 464³; sec. 517; sec. 528; sec. 543³; sec. 544³.

Laws of 1821, c. 211; 1823, c. 138; 1825, c. 324.

1833, c. 11²; 1834, c. 199.

1840, c. 311; 1841, c. 276; 1844, c. 105; c. 273; c. 315; 1845, c. 192³; 1847, c. 280, sec. 16; c. 470, sec. 27; 1848, c. 37; c. 153; 1849, c. 121; c. 226; c. 306.

1850, c. 102; c. 283; 1851, c. 180; c. 272; 1852, c. 53; c. 73; *c. 374;* 1853, c. 183; c. 217³; c. 238; c. 283; c. 352³; 1854, c. 96; c. 127; 1855, c. 86; c. 337; 1857, c. 344, sec. 34; c. 446³; c. 628²; 1858, c. 17²; c. 279; c. 332; 1859, c. 70³.

1860, c. 16; *1861, c. 31;* c. 158; c. 210; 1862, c. 412; c. 460; 1865, c. 612; 1867, c. 260; 1868, c. 828²; 1869, c. 856²; c. 883.

1870, c. 47; c. 81, sec. 214; c. 129; c. 263³; c. 519, tit. 3, sec. 7; c. 741; 1871, c. 57; c. 859; 1872, c. 475²; *c. 629;* c. 838; *1873, c. 239;* c. 330²; c. 370; c. 427²; c. 538; 1874, c. 192; c. 312; c. 322; c. 628; c. 656; 1875, c. 91; c. 166; c. 479; 1876, c. 196; c. 439; 1877, c. 11; c. 167; c. 387; 1878, c. 186²; 1879, c. 53, sec. 62²; c. 390.

1880, c. 344; c. 354; 1881, c. 182²; *c. 532;* c. 682; 1882, c. 360; *c. 410, sec. 1103;* 1883, c. 299, sec. 7; c. 309; 1886, c. 120, sec. 76; c. 672; 1887, c. 554, tit. 5, sec. 1; 1888, c. 577; 1889, c. 125.

1891, c. 208²; *1892, c. 182;* c. 342; 1893, c. 104; c. 204; c. 279; c. 416²; c. 721²; 1895, c. 565, sec. 83³; c. 601; 1896, c. 243; c. 378; c. 559; c. 853; 1897, c. 378 (Gr. N. Y. Charter), chap. 20, tit. 2, sec. 1351; *sec. 1364;* sec. 1370; c. 383; c. 414, sec. 182; 1898, c. 199³; *1899, c. 34;* c. 289³.

1900, c. 252; *1901, c. 602;* 1903, c. 41; 1908, c. 503, sec. 233; 1911, c. 856.

Unconstitutional

Rev. Stat., vol. 1, p. 638, sec. 1.

Code Proc., *sec. 30;* sec. 69.

Code Civ. Proc., sec. 263; *sec. 791²; sec. 793²;* sec. 920; sec. 1440²; sec. 1759²; sec. 3226.

Laws of 1824, c. 266²; 1825, c. 181².

1840, c. 311; 1849, c. 28; c. 140.

1850, c. 295; 1852, c. 374; 1853, c. 217; 1859, c. 10.

1860, c. 449, sec. 4; *1861, c. 31;* 1866, c. 217; 1869, c. 569.

1870, c. 382; c. 383, sec. 49; c. 467; 1871, c. 282; c. 383, sec. 49; *1872, c. 629²;* c. 700; *1873, c. 239;* 1874, c. 171²; c. 545²; 1876, c. 193; c. 196; 1878, c. 186².

1880, c. 265²; c. 480; 1881, c. 415; *c. 532;* c. 564; c. 681²; *1882, c. 410, sec. 1103;* 1886, c. 418; 1887, c. 384²; c. 452²; c. 557.

1890, c. 56; c. 58, tit. 7, sec. 11; c. 561, sec. 29; c. 742²; *1892, c. 182;* c. 664; 1895, c. 342; 1896, c. 22; 1897, c. 378 (Gr. N. Y. Charter), *sec. 1364;* sec. 1392; c. 417, sec. 7; *1899, c. 34;* c. 587.

1901, c. 466; *c. 602;* 1902, c. 532²; 1904, c. 598; 1907, c. 603; c. 751, sec. 349.

LOCAL AND PRIVATE

Constitutional

Rev. Stat., vol. 1, p. 452.

Laws of 1805, p. 126; 1806, c. 78³.

1815, c. 89³; 1816, c. 56³.

1851, c. 100²; 1852, c. 9; 1853, c. 204; c. 257²; c. 442; 1855, c. 347; 1857, c. 14; 1859, c. 392.

1863, c. 361, sec. 9; 1864, c. 303²; 1865, c. 233²; 1866, c. 576; 1867, c. 96; c. 353; 1868, c. 816.

1870, c. 767; 1871, c. 5; c. 301; c. 715; 1872, c. 639; 1873, c. 84; 1875, c. 257; 1877, c. 169; c. 459²; 1879, c. 467².

1881, c. 13; 1885, c. 238; c. 428; 1886, c. 472; 1888, c. 541; 1889, c. 17.

1890, c. 276; c. 393; 1893, c. 522; 1897, c. 378 (Gr. N. Y. Charter), chap. 17, tit. 4; 1898, c. 576.

1900, c. 767; 1901, c. 89; c. 402; 1908, c. 466.

Unconstitutional

Laws of 1807, c. 114.

1837, c. 62².

1840, c. 160; 1848, c. 76; 1849, c. 112².

1863, c. 361, sec. 9; 1864, c. 191; 1865, c. 181; 1868, c. 254; c. 577; c. 864²; 1869, c. 282².

1871, c. 706; 1872, c. 23.

1881, c. 13; c. 637; 1885, c. 377; 1886, c. 244; c. 510.

1891, c. 42; 1895, c. 167; 1896, c. 141; c. 448; 1899, c. 614; c. 700.

1900, c. 252; c. 614.

PUBLIC SERVICE

Constitutional

Code Civ. Proc., sec. 3379.

Laws of 1826, c. 253.

1831, c. 43; 1839, c. 218.

1840, c. 193; 1847, c. 31; 1848, c. 154; c. 358; 1849, c. 284.

1850, c. 111; *c. 140²;* c. 158; c. 215; 1851, c. 389, secs. 285–292; c. 497; 1852, c. 375; 1854, c. 63; *c. 271; c. 282²;* 1855, c. 545; 1856, c. 64; *1857, c. 156.*

1860, c. 513; *1863, c. 361;* 1866, c. 633⁵; 1867, c. 393; c. 846; c. 962⁵; 1868, c. 842; 1869, c. 237; c. 260; c. 907.

1870, c. 70⁵; 1871, c. 574; 1872, c. 594; c. 702; 1873, c. 531²; c. 647; c. 737³; 1874, c. 430²; c. 448²; c. 478; c. 648; 1875, c. 249; c. 422; c. 595;

c. 600; c. 606; 1876, c. 187; c. 415³; 1877, c. 64⁵; 1879, c. 89⁵.

1880, c. 191; *c. 582;* 1881, c. 321³; 1882, c. 259; 1884, c. 252, sec. 14; c. 439; c. 534³; 1885, c. 499³; 1886, c. 163; c. 268; 1887, c. 716³; 1888, c. 583²; 1889, c. 236²; c. 531.

1890, c. 565, sec. 78; sec. 91²; secs. 93–105; sec. 102²; *1891, c. 59;* c. 245²; c. 259; 1892, c. 151; c. 306³; c. 339; c. 340; c. 676³; 1893, c. 225; c. 239; c. 434³; 1894, c. 693²; 1895, c. 545²; *c. 1027²;* 1896, c. 338; c. 649; c. 835²; 1897, c. 754.

1901, c. 466; 1905, c. 357; c. 358; c. 629³; c. 630³; c. 631³; *c. 737;* 1907, c. 428.

Unconstitutional

Laws of 1850, *c. 140;* 1852, c. 356; *1854, c. 271; c. 282; 1857, c. 156, sec. 12;* 1858, c. 266².

1860, c. 258²; *1863, c. 361;* 1867, c. 489²; 1868, c. 334.

1870, c. 282; 1873, c. 185³; c. 452; 1874, c. 503³; 1876, c. 66; 1878, c. 206.

1880, c. 577; *c. 582;* 1881, c. 454³; 1885, c. 554²; 1886, c. 271; c. 312.

1891, c. 59; 1893, c. 459; 1894, c. 719; 1895, c. 417; *c. 1027;* 1898, c. 151.

1905, c. 737.

SOCIAL AND ECONOMIC

Constitutional

Rev. Laws, vol. 1, p. 339; vol. 2, p. 445, sec. 267.

Rev. Stat., vol. 1, p. 452; p. 603, sec. 5; p. 665, sec. 28; p. 666, sec. 29; p. 677; p. 678, sec. 6; vol. 2, p. 1008, sec. 2; sec. 3.

Code Civ. Proc., sec. 382²; sec. 414²; sec. 1582³; sec. 1780; sec. 2323a; secs. 2706–2714.

Code Crim. Proc., sec. 3; sec. 308; sec. 371; sec. 392; sec. 454.

Penal Code, sec. 12²; sec. 41q; sec. 79; sec. 265; sec. 267; sec. 292; secs. 334 a-b; sec. 364a; sec. 383; sec. 384h; sec. 550²; sec. 675; sec. 688.

Penal Law, sec. 1340.

Laws of 1805, c. 98.

1816, c. 1; 1817, c. 137; 1818, c. 259.

1821, c. 19.

1830, c. 291²; 1833, c. 300²; 1834, c. 37²; 1836, c. 242²; 1837, c. 430; 1838, c. 266.

1841, c. 168²; 1843, c. 169²; 1845, c. 115; 1846, c. 274; 1847, c. 450²; 1848, c. 40; c. 200²; 1849, c. 226; c. 375².

1850, c. 82; 1851, c. 151; c. 513; 1852, c. 361; c. 384; 1853, c. 539; 1854, c. 402; 1855, c. 428; 1857, c. 446, sec. 52; c. 628; 1858, c. 338.

1860, c. 202; c. 501; c. 508; 1861, c. 173; 1862, c. 63, sec. 39; c. 459²; c. 482; 1866, c. 466; c. 578; 1867, c. 628; c. 814²; 1869, c. 678; c. 834; c. 885; c. 888².

1870, c. 78²; c. 704; 1871, c. 57; c. 303²; c. 721; 1872, c. 580; c. 836; 1873, c. 357; c. 505, sec. 51; c. 549; c. 646; 1874, c. 209; c. 446; 1875, c. 79; c. 633²; 1876, c. 122; c. 431; 1877, c. 466²; 1878, c. 315²; 1879, c. 153.

1880, c. 14, sec. 40, ¶21²; c. 14, sec. 218; c. 36²; c. 254; c. 456; c. 545²; c. 591²; 1881, c. 42²; c. 87; c. 187²; c. 700; 1882, c. 287; c. 294; c. 410, sec. 663; 1883, c. 205; c. 317²; c. 336²; 1884, c. 202; c. 438²; 1885, c. 183; c. 342; c. 405; 1886, c. 21; c. 141; c. 271²; c. 310²; c. 572; 1887, c. 17²; c. 84; c. 377²; c. 479; 1888, c. 181²; c. 489; c. 555²; c. 581; 1889, c. 39³; c. 40³; c. 282; c. 380; c. 385; c. 515.

1890, c. 400; c. 401; c. 564, sec. 55; c. 568; 1891, c. 105, tit. 24, sec. 504; 1892, c. 182, sec. 164;

c. 602^2; c. 646; c. 686, secs. 125–126; c. 689, sec. 52; c. 711; 1893, c. 189; c. 279^2; c. 338, sec. 22^2; c. 338, sec. 32^2; c. 352; c. 661, sec. 24; c. 661, secs. 140, 153; c. 661, sec. 200; 1894, c. 28, sec. 9^2; c. 115^3; c. 317, secs. 90–95^2; 1895, c. 283; c. 398^2; c. 412^3; *c. 570;* c. 572; c. 823; 1896, c. 112, sec. 3; c. 112, sec. 31c; c. 112, sec. 31e; c. 378; c. 448; c. 545, sec. 62^2; c. 850; 1897, c. 377^2; c. 415; 1898, c. 122; c. 181^2; c. 422; 1899, c. 385; c. 515; c. 690. 1900, c. 20^4; c. 327, sec. 45^2; c. 667, secs. 194, 199–201; 1901, c. 466, sec. 707a; c. 466, sec. 1172; 1902, c. 194^4; c. 317^4; c. 495^3; c. 572, sec. 30; c. 600; 1903, c. 132; c. 146^2; c. 326^2; 1904, c. 569; c. 588^4; *1905, c. 241;* c. 582; c. 602^2; c. 603^2; 1906, c. 314; c. 326; c. 440; c. 506; 1907, c. 185; c. 344; 1908, c. 144; *c. 429;* 1909, c. 9, sec. 41; c. 36, sec. 7a; c. 36, secs. 10–12; c. 49; 1910, c. 607.

Unconstitutional

Rev. Stat., vol. 2, p. 548.

Code Civ. Proc., sec. 1582^2; sec. 1759^2.

Penal Code, sec. 41x; sec. 171a; sec. 335a^2; sec. 342; sec. 384p^2; sec. 384q^2; secs. 615–616^2; sec. 640, ¶ 16^2; sec. 640d^2.

Laws of 1848, *c. 200.*

1855, c. 164; c. 231.

1862, c. 459; 1866, c. 466; 1867, c. 372.

1870, c. 394.

1880, c. 59; 1882, c. 410, secs. 663–666; 1883, c. 93; *c. 205;* c. 317; 1884, c. 60; c. 202; c. 272; 1886, c. 310; 1887, c. 377^2; c. 401^2; c. 479; c. 691^2; 1888, c. 181^2; c. 543; c. 555, sec. 6a^3; c. 583, tit. 14, sec. 51; *1889, c. 39.*

1890, c. 25^2; c. 163; 1891, c. 364^2; 1893, c. 338, sec. 27^2; c. 452^2; 1894, c. 498^3; c. 623; 1895, c. 384; *c. 570;* c. 572^3; c. 635, tit. 12, sec. 3; 1896, c. 112, sec. 28^2; c. 383; c. 448; c. 529, sec. 82; c. 547, sec.

83^2; c. 803; c. 908, sec. 321^3; c. 931; 1897, c. 281; c. 378 (Gr. N. Y. Charter), sec. 610; secs. 707–711; sec. 1501; c. 415, sec. 3^3; c. 506^2; 1898, c. 151; 1899, c. 192^3; c. 567^3; c. 700.

1900, c. 534^2; c. 725; c. 742^2; c. 768^2; 1901, c. 128^2; c. 640^2; 1902, c. 528; 1903, c. 184, sec. 77; c. 272^2; 1904, c. 657^2; *1905, c. 241^3;* c. 572; 1906, c. 502; 1907, c. 185; c. 324; 1908, c. 350; *c. 429;* 1909, c. 29, sec. 85; c. 400; 1910, c. 374, sec. 290; c. 674.

TAXES AND ASSESSMENTS

Constitutional

A. Taxes

Rev. Stat., vol. 1, p. 398, sec. 2; p. 714^4.
Laws of 1813, c. 86^2.

1837, c. 30^4.

1843, c. 230; 1846, c. 327; 1849, c. 178^4.

1850, c. 84; c. 183; 1851, c. 176; 1852, c. 8; 1855, c. 327; c. 335; c. 427; 1857, c. 548^4.

1861, c. 143, sec. 86; c. 308; 1863, c. 15; 1865, c. 97; c. 215; c. 453; c. 694; c. 761; 1867, c. 96; 1869, c. 855; c. 875; c. 876.

1870, c. 137; 1872, c. 836; 1873, c. 119; c. 643; c. 647; 1874, c. 180; 1875, c. 60^2; c. 482^2; 1879, c. 382^3.

1880, c. 542^2; 1881, c. 361^2; c. 402^3; 1882, c. 287; c. 363; c. 383; c. 410, sec. 523; 1883, c. 21; c. 114^2; c. 298; c. 516^3; 1884, c. 153^2; 1885, c. 163^2; c. 215^2; c. 448; c. 483; 1886, c. 143; c. 224; c. 656; 1887, c. 713; 1889, c. 311.

1892, c. 143, sec. 68; 1896, c. 112, sec. 28; c. 908, secs. 1, 3; c. 908, sec. 141^2; 1897, c. 312^2; c. 392^2· 1899, c. 128; c. 712.

1905, c. 241; c. 729; 1907, c. 721.

B. *Assessments*

Laws of 1818, c. 210².

1834, c. 92; 1835, c. 309.

1841, c. 171².

1852, c. 293; 1859, c. 484².

1860, c. 100²; 1861, c. 297²; 1863, c. 196; 1867, c. 360, sec. 25; 1868, c. 460; c. 631²; 1869, c. 383².

1872, c. 580²; c. 741; c. 812; 1873, c. 387, sec. 18; 1874, c. 287; c. 588²; 1875, c. 369; c. 633, tit. 12, sec. 13.

1881, c. 554; c. 689; 1885, c. 131, sec. 90; 1886, c. 622; 1887, c. 136.

1892, c. 289²; 1895, c. 817; 1897, c. 324.

1901, c. 28²; c. 133²; c. 466, sec. 973; 1905, c. 676; 1907, c. 91.

Unconstitutional

A. *Taxes*

Laws of 1841, c. 341.

1872, c. 734.

1887, c. 627.

1906, c. 414.

B. *Assessments*

Laws of 1844, c. 86; 1846, c. 133²; 1847, c. 375².

1850, c. 262; 1859, c. 396, sec. 24.

1868, c. 314²; c. 673, tit. 2, sec. 13; 1869, c. 217².

1870, c. 608; c. 619²; 1871, c. 461, tit. 10; 1872, c. 715²; 1878, c. 277.

1880, c. 114; 1882, c. 393; 1883, c. 523, secs. 126–127; 1886, c. 656.

1901, c. 200²; c. 719².

The Riverside Press

CAMBRIDGE · MASSACHUSETTS

U · S · A

Removed for first time
7/20/64 until 7/23-1964